Michael,

FROM
MY BAD
TO
MY BEST

Wishing you The Best.....

Always!,

Julii

FROM
MY BAD
TO
MY BEST

HOW INDIVIDUALS AND COMPANIES

CAN **DIFFERENTIATE** THEMSELVES

IN THE AGE OF MEDIOCRATY
                                    I

(oops, My Bad... Mediocrity)

JULIE B. KAMPF

FOREWORD BY ERNIE ANASTOS
AUTHOR AND DISTINGUISHED EMMY AWARD–WINNING TV NEWS ANCHOR

CAPTIVATING PRODUCTIONS LLC
ENGLEWOOD CLIFFS, NJ

Published by
Captivating Productions LLC
Englewood Cliffs, NJ

Publisher's Cataloging-in-Publication Data
Kampf, Julie B.

From my bad to my best : how individuals and companies can differentiate themselves in the age of mediocrity / Julie B. Kampf. – Englewood Cliffs, NJ : Captivating Productions LLC, 2014.

p. ; cm.

ISBN13: 978-0-9860807-0-8

1. Customer services. 2. Success in business. I. Title.

HF5415.5.K36 2014
658.812—dc23   2014947836

FIRST EDITION

Project coordination by Jenkins Group, Inc.
www.BookPublishing.com

Interior design by Brooke Camfield

Printed in the United States of America
18   17   16   15   14   •   5   4   3   2   1

Contents

Foreword

In a more innocent, less connected time—which was not that long ago—we behaved better, and there were fewer eyes and ears peeled to catch us if we did not. Our societal admonitions not to talk behind another's back and not to say certain things "in mixed company" were commonly honored. We were more polite, more courteous, and, even before the decidedly mixed blessing of political correctness arrived to keep us on our toes, more respectful to the diverse sensitivities of those around us.

This was true at home with our families, in public with both friends and strangers, and at work in the company of those colleagues and customers who occupy a substantial portion of our lives. It is this latter environment, the workplace that Julie Kampf takes on in *From My Bad to My Best* for its rampant and damaging incivility, which costs our society hundreds of billions of dollars and exacts from our fellow human beings an uncountable personal toll.

As *From My Bad to My Best* notes, 95 percent of Americans believe we have a civility problem, and 70 percent say it has become a crisis. Ninety-six percent experience incivility in the workplace, and they react in various negative ways, which include behaving with incivility themselves, resentfully underperforming at their jobs, or using their time to find a better place to work. Yet, studies show that when workers are treated in a civil manner, they work harder, and when customers are given the proper courtesy and respect, they come back.

I recently had the opportunity to reflect on the need for workplace civility when I was asked to give a speech on civility in journalism. For the past four decades, my workplace has been the newsroom, and in front of cameras and microphones, doing my job in the company of the fellow journalists and teammates who make possible the business of broadcast news and before millions of viewers who depend upon the accuracy, truth, and fairness that are the very foundations of my profession.

In my business, when we hit the air and go into millions of homes, it has to be with respect for those who watch and listen. We must be careful not to offend in any way and always aware of the trust placed in us. In the early days of broadcasting, we were civil to a fault. Edward R. Murrow would refer to members of his reporting staff at CBS as "Mr. Collingwood" or "Mr. Sevareid"—civility, with a touch of dignity that showed the kind of respectful, standards-observant society that we were.

Even today, most newspeople understand that their vital institution should reflect the best in American civility. They acknowledge each other's work, thank colleagues for their good reporting, and strive to deliver full, fair, and complete stories that help people live their lives.

Beyond the traditional newsroom, the public forum has been greatly expanded by new media and social media, and in some ways that's a wonderful thing for our society and democracy. It gives everyone a voice and the opportunity to express an opinion on the problems and issues of the day. But it has also allowed people to hide behind made-up screen names and peck hatefully and anonymously at the keyboards on their laptops and smartphones. Today, many people hurl insults at each other and question each other's motives and integrity in blogs and comments on newspaper stories and in 140-character invective-filled "tweets" without identifying themselves and taking responsibility for their words. As a result, our public discourse has become less respectful and far less civil.

There are many factors that no doubt have led to our increased lack of civility—political disagreement, economic disruptions and unemployment, the trend away from family life and religious practice, and "entertainment" such as reality shows and video games that encourage bad behavior, unhealthy habits, and the abandonment of values we once held dear. And though it would be difficult to pinpoint a specific time when our country and its manners changed so drastically, I think many of us will agree that the spread of the Internet as a playground for rumor mongers, hateful bloggers, and cyberbullies has given this awful trend its critical mass. Worst of all, many people just don't seem to care.

As Julie Kampf notes, "Something in our culture has made rudeness OK"—though we know, deep down, that it is not. In *From My Bad to My Best*, she tells us exactly how and why it is not OK and how we can better ourselves and our workplaces, reinventing a future with more "Please" and "Thank you," more "I'm sorry," and more "How can I help you?"

This very important book defines for the workplace a restored culture of civility, one that must succeed if we as a society are to succeed. We have a long distance to go—because we have come so far from where we belong—and it will not be easy, but *From My Bad to My Best* shows us the way.

—Ernie Anastos

Acknowledgments

As we express our gratitude, we must never forget that the highest appreciation is not to utter words, but to live by them.

—John F. Kennedy

It's rare that people have the opportunity in a public forum to thank those who mean a great deal to them. Writing a book may be one of the few times we might have that chance, and so I'd like to express my gratitude to a multitude of people who have loved and/or supported me on my journey.

Thank you:

To my parents, Audrey (may she rest in peace) and David, who have always been the greatest source of love and guidance. To my husband, Andy, who has given me the gift of a great partnership and provided me with unconditional love. To my son, Adam, who gives me joy and of whom I am so proud (Mama Bear loves you!). To my brother, Jeffrey, who has brought me to a healthier place in life. And to the rest of my family and wonderful friends whom I love and adore (you know who you are), thank you for being there for me always; I am so grateful.

To my colleagues at JBK Associates International, who provide me with the opportunity to do what I love with people I love; working with you is a gift. To my clients who make it possible every day for me to engage in helping your companies grow and flourish while we grow, I send you my sincerest thanks for your support, partnership, and confidence.

To those who helped me bring this work to life, especially Elizabeth King: you were my rock! Thanks to Jerry, Leah, Marcia, Yvonne, and Devon . . . looking forward to the next one!

To my advisors, Bob, Janet, Jane, Gene, and Keith, thank you for all you have done to help and be my guardrails.

And last but not least, to those who acknowledge the importance of this book, my thanks to Ernie Anastos, Leslie Voth, Jon Luther, Cindi Bigelow, Ken Mandelbaum, and Steve Grossberg. Your support of this message is hopefully the start of a great dialogue that is so necessary.

I express my gratitude to all who have helped me get to this milestone of my life, one that has been on my " A" goal list for way too long.

—Julie B. Kampf

Introduction

Don't apologize for anything.
Apologies are the antithesis of ass-covering.

—Stanley Bing

How many times a day do you hear the words "my bad"?

Someone's just forgotten a phone call, blown a deadline, missed a meeting that you've blocked on your calendar . . . the list continues. Almost no one says "I'm sorry" anymore. Now you get "my bad."

Welcome to "the Mediocre Revolution." The mind-set of "my bad" has taken over, and the first casualty is accountability. The Urban Dictionary defines "my bad" as "a way of admitting a mistake, and apologizing for that mistake, *without actually apologizing*" (italics mine). When you hear those two words, you can bet you've just been attacked by mediocrity. In fact, "my bad" could be the motto of the Mediocre Revolution.

No one escapes. You can see this mind-set in the chipped cup that's served with the tea you ordered 45 minutes ago and in the flight attendant who looks like he's not up for the challenge of providing you with a great customer experience. It's in the antics of the reality TV stars who we treat like heroes and the politicians who find new ways to define "shameless." In my line of work, helping companies with their executive talent, it's in the attitude of some hiring teams that figure their top choices will wait around no matter what and in the job candidate who gives a video interview with her head nodding closer and closer to the desk, where she looks like she's ready to take a nice nap.

These little things aren't small at all when you consider the costs. Just the stress caused by mundane slights and disrespect costs an estimated $300 billion a year in lost productivity. Costs rise from there as the mind-set of "my bad" kills service, quality, and trust. I see it every day. No one does business on a handshake anymore. Executives act as if they're above common courtesy, businesses treat employees like throwaways, and customers get lousy service. No wonder so many companies struggle. In many cases, the lawyers are the ones making a killing.

I completely support a capitalist society, but I believe that the best way to a strong bottom line is through putting people first. It just makes more sense to make a ton of money because your customers and colleagues love what you're doing instead of trying to make money despite how you treat them.

"Brilliant, Ed! A slogan we can finally live up to!"

But every day I see businesses treat people badly, and I believe the situation is likely to get much worse. Shifting demographics mean that five generations soon will work side by side in U.S. companies, each with its own distinct sense of how to manage relationships, and conflict is almost a given even in the rare places where colleagues go out of their way to treat each other with respect. Add in the cultural challenges of a global workforce and the opportunities for misunderstanding multiply. On top of that, every year, technological advances designed to make our lives easier also create new ways for us to be rude to each other, whether we're multitasking during a virtual meeting or sending an abrupt text (probably while multitasking during our meeting) or hitting the dreaded "reply all."

Rehumanizing the workplace will only get tougher as the pace of business quickens, the pressure to be always "on" increases, and everyone knows that you can work 19 hours a day and still get beaten by a competitor who works 20. It hardly helps when employers take the attitude of "If you don't like it here, you can go somewhere else" and employees act like they're wondering "So what have you done for me lately?" But building relationships is also more important than ever, and that starts with human relationships. Eventually, everybody will have access to the same technology. What will set companies apart, and help them beat the competition, is talent.

With all this in mind, after three decades of closely watching the best and worst of how people interact in business, I offer my scientific opinion. Companies don't have to crush their people. Customers don't have to get crushed. It's pretty much that simple.

I wrote this book to show businesses how to get a grip in a world where mediocrity has become more the norm than the exception, and I know this because it's a topic of discussion quite often these days. Everyone knows it exists; the question becomes, What can we do about it? Some have given up, others have taken the attitude of "If you can't beat 'em, join 'em," and still others like me are trying to spread the word that we must shift behaviors and reevaluate what is acceptable. I have a problem with paying for something and feeling bad that I wasn't given the utmost attention or quality, whether it's a product or a service. The pages ahead will take a look at the "my bad" mind-set and how to get past it, from the basic indifferences we suffer in the course of daily life, to the behavior of our popular and political leaders, to the changing standards of service, to the way the Mediocre Revolution plays out in business, at home, and with our kids. We'll also consider causes for hope.

As alarming as current trends are, we don't have to change the universe today in order to avoid collapsing like the Roman Empire. Let's start by having a conversation about how to do better. Many of us care about principles such as quality, integrity, and customer service, but we get so caught up in day-to-day pressures and a climate of lower standards that we don't follow through. The more we talk about why these principles matter, the more likely we are to put them into action. That can even mean small adjustments. We just might beat the Mediocre Revolution together by fighting the little battles that the forces of mediocrity want us to ignore. Do the simple things differently. Say "I'm sorry." Answer e-mails. Keep your head off the desk when you're on Skype. It may seem like common sense; it just doesn't seem to be commonplace . . . a reoccurring thought that stays with me.

For now, every time I hear "my bad," I think I understand what NCAA champion women's basketball coach Geno Auriemma was getting at when he explained that he yells from the sidelines because he gets frustrated seeing players do dumb stuff. "My bad" and things like it are dumb stuff, and this book is my way of yelling from the sidelines.

1

No "Thank-you"

We plan that this would result in an estimated reduction of 12,500 factory direct and professional employees over the next year.

—Stephen Elop, Microsoft's executive VP of devices and services, announcing layoffs to employees in paragraph 11 of a corporate strategy memo

Recently, while I was at the theater, someone held the door open for me. I did a double take because I can't remember the last time that happened. Then, a few days later, a drugstore clerk asked, "Is there anything else we can help you with?" I felt like I'd hit the lottery. One of my colleagues was speechless when he went to return a humidifier to the store where he purchased it and the sales manager took it back, no questions asked, and gave him a new one. Speechless? Isn't that what customer service is about, serving the customer?

Here's what's even more astounding. A recent local awards dinner I attended featured a nationally recognized emcee who makes regular appearances on TV news and talk shows. That mediagenic emcee mangled one recipient's name after another, as if she hadn't even looked at the script, while the poor hosts who tried to honor people who do great work for the community looked on. Go to any local awards dinner and count the number of names the presenter mispronounces. Or watch the Oscars and see it broadcast worldwide. At most events these days, you could almost make a list of common mispronunciations and use it to start up a game of Botched Name Bingo.

Something in our culture has made rudeness OK—better than OK: it's even rewarded! The Real Housewives have a fistfight, and we all want to watch. Comic Zach Galifianakis says that rudeness is hilarious and becomes popular enough to score an interview with President Obama. We all feel what's happening. Ninety-five percent of Americans think we have a civility problem in this country and 70 percent say incivility has reached crisis levels, according to the 2013 Civility in America survey conducted by the public relations firm Weber Shandwick and public affairs firm Powell Tate. The business world has joined in, and rude treatment in the office is nearly universal. Ninety-six percent of people experience incivility at work, according to research from business school professors Christine Pearson and Christine Porath, authors of the book *The Cost of Bad Behavior: How Incivility Is Damaging Your Business and What to Do about It.*

A $300-BILLION BUSINESS PROBLEM

It's easy to dismiss workplace civility as a warm and fuzzy "nice-to-have"—until you look at the business costs of doing without it. Every day, "mundane"

2

slights and disrespect cause stress that costs U.S. companies $300 billion a year, according to Pearson and Porath.

Consider a few of those costs. For starters, businesses pay the turnover costs for employees who quit their jobs to escape incivility. That's not just a few disgruntled people. More than one in four Americans has quit a job because it was an uncivil workplace, according to the Civility in America survey. If you figure that replacing a supervisor or manager today typically costs about 1.5 times that person's salary and replacing an executive costs 2.5 times his or her salary, you can see how quickly turnover costs add up. Here's the catch: as an employer, you may never know how much talent and money you're losing to incivility. It's not the kind of thing departing employees typically share in exit interviews.

I see talented executives leave their positions all the time when corporations have the mentality that "if you don't like it here, leave and find another job." Executives placed by our firm, JBK Associates International (JBK), rarely leave within the first couple of years—we have a 92 percent candidate retention rate, averaging at least three years after hire—but we once saw a fantastic, well-skilled executive quit after 90 days because he had no interest in working for someone who sat at a desk and barked orders all day and delivered nonstop verbal abuse. He found another great role immediately. That's no surprise: top talent always has options, even in a tough economy. His former employer had a harder time filling his role, which was of little surprise considering that companies that treat their people with disrespect quickly earn a reputation that makes recruiting a challenge.

I see how this trend plays out with the firms that my company supports. The less civil the culture is, the tougher it is to fill a position quickly—and, of course, unfilled positions cost employers money. Some companies provide a collaborative, team-based environment that allows for interaction and great outcomes. That makes it easy for our team to answer the first question candidates typically ask recruiters: "What's the culture like?" It also makes it easier for our team to deliver a qualified, diverse slate of candidates with top speed.

Other client companies have such intense cultures that we have to drag candidates kicking and screaming to interview for a great opportunity. I know that a client is in trouble when candidates refuse even to explore an opportunity by telling us, "I've heard too much about this company."

As it turns out, turnover and recruitment costs are just the start of what businesses lose to incivility. Many employees don't quit when they encounter incivility; they stay and demolish productivity. Imagine being so angry with an employer that you do less work on purpose. That's what happens with nearly half of people targeted by incivility in the workplace, according to a study Pearson and Porath conducted and reported in their book. Most other employees who stay don't work less intentionally; they simply allow their performance to decline as their commitment to the organization declines. Maybe they're a little less likely to respond immediately to every urgent e-mail, a little more likely to take all their sick days, and a lot more likely to focus their best energy on creating CYA ("cover your a**") documentation.

Add to the costs of lost productivity the costs of lost business when incivility makes its way to customers. Pearson and Porath say that more than 15 percent of incivility targets purposely decreased customer civility after experiencing incivility from a coworker. More often, a rude workplace culture simply turns customers into collateral damage. Small acts of rudeness can drive customers away. I know I won't return to a luxury goods store that will remain nameless but that acted like I wasn't good enough to buy its products, and I'm not so sure I want to give my hard-earned money to any organization whose receptionist gives me the cold shoulder when I visit someone to discuss my money, my health, etc. We experience this every day and perhaps have become somewhat oblivious to it, but I find it extremely distasteful.

As workplace problems grow, consequences become more serious. I don't think it's a coincidence that an automaker that received a record penalty for a decade-long product recall delay also had a reputation for a culture of intimidation. When I read that a former executive described red flags such as getting ridiculed in meetings and ego-driven CEOs who had no problem making employees look bad, it became easy to see how customer safety could get lost.

Even if you've been able to avoid having managers who deliver abuse to subordinates—and if you have, congratulations—your business is still vulnerable to incivility-driven losses. Resentment can build even from small workplace infractions such as saying please and thank-you, neglecting workplace upkeep, and making excessive noise, according to a 2010 *Business Management Daily* column. Think of all the habits coworkers have that annoy you—the chronic lateness, loud personal calls, odorous food, tendency to mark routine e-mails as urgent, repeatedly hitting you up for their kid's fundraiser, cheerfully skipping out for a haircut while the rest of the team works late on a tight deadline, even the innocent verbal tics or the overuse of all caps—and then ask yourself how many annoying habits you may have. Add together all the time you spend being annoyed and venting to calm down and all the time they probably spend doing the same thing. That probably represents a significant loss in productivity.

Of course, employers don't create a climate of incivility by themselves. Job candidates have their own issues with basic manners. Last week I got up at 5 a.m. and drove about 45 miles to take a candidate to breakfast. She waited more than 48 hours to thank me for my time and show me that she was really interested in the position. I am a complete believer that candidates must show they are really passionate about what they do and want to work for the company. To me, this person's actions say that she's probably not going to succeed in an organization that prioritizes treating people with respect.

I see incivility getting worse on both sides. In some job interviews, I feel like I can count the seconds until the candidate asks about salary. My husband, who is also in the staffing industry, has seen even worse. He recently called a consultant to share valuable feedback that was provided by his employer and discuss the go-forward plan. The person did not agree that the feedback was valid and with that . . . he hung up on my husband. A company that hires someone with civility issues soon sees that "desk rage" is a real phenomenon as instances of yelling, tantrums, and even equipment damage multiply. When incivility becomes bullying, costs get steeper. For employers, workplace bullying costs an estimated $64–$300 billion per year, according to Patricia G. Barnes, J.D., author of *Surviving Bullies, Queen Bees, and Psychopaths in the Workplace.*

For employees, the rude treatment often starts even before the job offer arrives. We have been told stories of candidates who fly to interviews only to arrive and find out the meeting was canceled, the schedules were changed, or people who were supposed to be on the interview slates didn't show up for the meeting. What message does that send to an executive with the skills to help your company grow? Even if a candidate succeeds in the interview, he or she may wait for months and months without a word of response from the interviewer as more employers extend the hiring process.

Once the job starts, people face stresses that would have been unimaginable when baby boomers (such as me) started our careers. No one's job is safe in an era that has made layoffs and reorganizations routine and terminations increasingly brutal. Among other things, you now can get fired via conference call, e-mail, or text. Just imagine dialing into a conference call with hundreds of fellow employees and hearing the words "Your role has been eliminated, and you will no longer have a role" and "Today will be your last day," as happened in 2014 to employees of the news service Patch in a move that *Fortune* magazine called "a punch to the gut." Or think of how Florida restaurant employees must have felt when they received a text saying that the restaurant was shutting down and they should not report to work. Those of you who have watched the television show *Sex and the City* may remember that Carrie Bradshaw once got dumped via a Post-it note. Whether the situation is romantic or professional, this is never an acceptable way to end a relationship.

It's hard to believe that things can get worse. In the world we live in now, politicians get shoes thrown at them, a congressman threatens to "break" a reporter "in half" and throw him off a balcony, and college students find feces in campus clothes dryers. When an Australian driver hit a bicyclist while she was texting, fracturing the spine of the victim, who then spent three months in the hospital, she told the police, "I just don't care" because her car is "pretty expensive and now I have to fix it."

In business, the pressures are only increasing, and so will the costs. More clashes are coming, as five generations soon will work side by side, the global economy forces collaboration among people of many different cultural backgrounds, the labor force becomes more diverse, and opinion becomes more polarized. In today's climate, I wonder how Democrats and Republicans will work together if another presidential election goes to the Supreme Court or how evangelicals and atheists will maintain civility as courts decide cases that pit religious liberty against inclusion.

I believe we face a choice: fight the Mediocre Revolution by taking simple steps to create a more respectful culture or surrender to incivility and accept serious losses to talent, productivity, and revenue. I say we fight.

SHOW CIVILITY—IT PAYS

As rudeness increases, we need to amp up the opposition. Research shows that nasty interactions have a fivefold-stronger effect on our mood than positive interactions. To me, that means we've got to counter every incivility with five courtesies. Here's a 10-step battle plan to help restore simple dignities to the workplace and protect business from the costs of rising incivility.

1. *Say Thank-You and Please*: A simple thank-you might increase employee effort by as much as 50 percent. Harvard Business School Professor Francesca Gino and Wharton School Professor Adam Gant studied 41 university fundraisers in research released in 2010. The school's director visited

half in person and told them, "I am very grateful for your hard work. We sincerely appreciate your contributions to the university." The second group received no such expressions of gratitude. Expressing gratitude increased the number of calls made by fundraisers by more than 50 percent for the week. Fundraisers who received no thanks made about the same number of calls as the previous week.

I believe that "please" can be similarly powerful. Donald McCullough, author of *Say Please, Say Thank You: The Respect We Owe One Another*, points out that "please" matters because it acknowledges the freedom of others and suggests that if you can't take half a second to say please, you don't deserve to have anyone do anything for you. I've read that a restaurant in Nice, France, cares so much about "please" that it instituted manners-based tiered pricing for coffee on the basis of how respectful each customer is to the staff. I don't know that I'd take it that far, but that restaurant might be on to something.

2. *Apologize Honestly*: If you've read this book's introduction, you've probably already guessed that the polite phrase that means the most to me is "I'm sorry." To me, that's one of the most powerful ways to show that you care—of course, as long as it's sincere. I still frequent a deli where I once found a hair in my sandwich because the owner was so clearly mortified and otherwise the restaurant has been so consistently excellent. In fact, as I write this book, my team has made a mistake. We sent the wrong version of a candidate's résumé to a client. We realized it quickly, apologized, and put a system in place so we won't make that mistake again. Our client has seen that we're not perfect and, importantly, has seen that we care deeply about excellence. As far as I'm concerned, when in doubt, apologize. And when you apologize, show sincerity, say what you did wrong, acknowledge that you caused harm, and commit to making amends or to making sure that it doesn't happen again.

3. *Return E-mails*: You should have a time limit in your mind for how long you'll wait before responding to an e-mail. I find it helpful to remember that, apart from spam, a human being is on the end of every e-mail in my box. I'm also inspired to read that, as Ford CEO, Alan Mulally had a habit of answering nearly every e-mail the day he received it and that Apple CEO Tim Cook loves to answer customer e-mails. If they can do it, so can I.

People who respond to me quickly and courteously have my goodwill even if they're delivering bad news. When my firm approached Zappos about doing business together, what the company calls a "ninja" got back to us within 24 hours with a polite no, thank you. Apparently, the popular online retailer receives 2,000 similar queries a day and answers every one. Now I want to shop with Zappos!

4. *Start Meetings on Time*: Some corporate cultures still view it as a sign of importance when executives act too busy to get to a meeting on time. Those businesses epitomize the Mediocre Revolution. In my experience, when a company's most senior executives commit to starting meetings promptly, on-time start times become part of the culture. If it helps, imagine the cost of the hour of staff time lost every time a six-person meeting starts 10 minutes late. Prompt start times build a more respectful culture by showing employees that their time matters.

5. *Eyes off the iPhone*: Texting during meetings is awful, and I've done it. If you're in a business with clients who need to hear back from you quickly, it's tough to sit in a meeting without checking your phone. But it's also annoying. A 2013 study from Pitney Bowes found that 54 percent of U.S. workers were irritated by business contacts who relentlessly check their phones and e-mails during meetings. My recommendation: for an hour-long meeting, put your phones away. For a longer meeting, establish parameters up front by telling the group how often there will be a break and asking them to stay off their phones in the meantime.

6. *"I Really Need to Take This Call"*: More than 30 years ago when I was a young executive, my boss took a personal phone call five minutes into an 8:30 a.m. meeting. Five, 10, 15 minutes went by, and I finally made a move to leave, motioning that I would return when she was off. The boss instantly pointed to the chair and ordered me to sit back down, as if to say, "Your time is not valuable." That has stuck with me all this time—I don't even want to think about the productivity I lost back then every time I thought about it. Just the fact that I remember it today speaks volumes. Sometimes interruptions can't be helped. Today, I try to show basic respect to the people around me by at least letting them know that I care. "I really need to take this call. Can we pick this up at a time that works for everyone?"

7. *Watch Your Tone*: Using a respectful tone makes delivering tough feedback much easier. You can convey the toughest information, disagree with gusto, and still show a respectful tone, even in an e-mail. It doesn't cost you anything. When you go to a meeting and lace into somebody who disagrees with you, using a respectful tone takes no more time than using an insulting one. When I was growing up, if I started to mouth off to my father, he would say, "When you want to speak with me properly, I'll be happy to talk to you." I'm certainly not perfect, and in truth I've given my share of attitude when feeling the pressure, but I do work to show respect to the people around me. I can see the results in the hard work my team puts in for the business.

8. *Make Respect a Priority*: I'd like to see every management team do an off-site where they talk about the organization's cultural goals and how to get there—and then they put that talk into action, starting at the top. The Society for Human Resources Management (SHRM) highlights Huntsville, Alabama, Company Intuitive Research and Technology Corp. for steps including a session called "Let's Talk Ethics with Hal," where the company's cofounder and president discusses ethical decisions and how important employee actions are to the company. The firm's HR director says of the cofounder, "His strength is that he means every word of it, and he shows it in how he lives every day in terms of running the company." Corporate Utopia doesn't exist, but basic respect can and still does when it's a priority. What it comes down to is prioritizing people and remembering that when everyone has access to technology, what sets an organization apart is talent. At the very least, think twice when you get the urge to send a colleague a cheerful e-card that says, "Your weight issue makes you look like you've been scraped out of a Crisco bucket." Don't think this hasn't happened; this is an actual e-card.

9. *Mind Your Digital Manners*: Digital rudeness hurts businesses and careers. When a Beverly Hills restaurant posted tweets "outing" customer no-shows, one of those no-shows went to the press to say that a relative had died 20 minutes before the reservation and that the customer would not be returning any time soon. Other businesses have been forced to fire employees for posts that were racist, sexist, or demeaning to customers.

Whether you get your next job could hinge on that insensitive post you made three years ago or the embarrassing photo in which you're tagged or even the mortifying e-mail you sent with "reply all." If you're a senior executive, your next employer will likely look at pretty much everything you've ever done on social media thanks to the increasing popularity of background searches by firms such as the corporate investigation and risk-consulting firm Kroll. The tweet you made in a moment of frustration—"I can't believe they're finally launching this stupid product"—will now probably cost you your job. So will an attempt at humor if it denigrates others. A communications executive started a long flight by putting out a supposedly humorous tweet with racist overtones, became an Internet sensation while in the air as the remark was retweeted more than 2,000 times, and lost her job soon after she landed.

Rudeness can stop your career faster than ever today. In 2014, the head of the Cleveland Job Bank started a firestorm on social media. A recent college graduate had contacted her to connect on LinkedIn and received a scathing response calling the invitation "tacky" and "inappropriate," saying "I love the sense of entitlement in your generation" and "You're welcome to your humility lesson for the year." The graduate posted the e-mail publicly, social media exploded, and the backlash was so strong that the executive agreed to give back her 2013 Communicator of the Year Award. A lesson: avoid the *e* word when talking with members of the Millennial generation, especially when you're picking a fight via social media. Just as you're "entitled" to your opinion, they're "entitled" to embarrass you by sharing it.

10. *Don't Confuse Toughness with Rudeness*: By all means, companies should have an intense culture with high demands and expectations and pressures. Give people the straight feedback they need when they're not up to par. Just remember that there's a difference between toughness and rudeness. Rudeness signals insecurity and hurts business. One of my firm's clients feels so strongly on this point that she gave me a plaque that I've kept on my desk for years. It says "Because Nice Matters."

Even years ago, businesses and executives paid a price for rudeness. Early in my career, when I worked in the fashion industry as an accessories merchandiser, I worked for a boss who was well known for bad behavior. Back when formal suits were the business standard, this boss showed up at a product review wearing a warm-up suit and responded to what our team thought was a strong presentation by throwing a wallet across the room and declaring "This sucks." No surprise: the company had high turnover, the bottom line eventually suffered, and eventually she was ousted. By treating people better, the boss might have avoided presiding over a corporate bankruptcy and getting fired. My takeaway: if you want to succeed, don't throw wallets or tantrums.

THE PAYOFF

Committing to civility doesn't mean creating Utopia or backing off from performance standards or trying to establish a workplace filled with people who hold hands and sing "Kumbaya" or act like characters from Disney. It means making respect a basic part of work life to generate a bottom-line payoff. The simple gestures that lead to a culture of respect often cost nothing more than a fraction of a second, but if enough of us make them at once, the potential payoff could be in the billions.

"We provide a working environment which nurtures that rare, creative spark found only between people who can't stand each other!"

CIVILITY AND THE BOTTOM LINE

Multiple studies suggest that increasing civility has bottom-line benefits well beyond the initial savings in turnover costs. A few highlights:

- With a more positively charged work environment, companies have higher profits via reduced turnover and increased customer satisfaction. In turn, a 1 percent increase in the service climate yields a 2 percent increase in revenue, according to research reported by Daniel Goleman, author of *Primal Leadership: Unleashing the Power of Emotional Intelligence.*

- Companies that maintain ethical workplace cultures are more financially successful and have more motivated, productive employees, according to research cited by the Society of Human Resource Management (SHRM).

- The annualized stock market returns of the *Fortune 100 Best Companies to Work For* in the United States were 11.8 percent compared with 6.4 percent for the Russell 3000 Index and 6 percent for the Standard & Poor's 500 index, according to the *Great Place to Work Institute.*

- Employees who feel welcome to express their authentic selves at work exhibit higher levels of individual performance, according to research by London Business School Professor Dan Cable.

CAREER-KILLING TWEETS

These people learned the hard way that things you would never say to your boss are probably also things you shouldn't tweet to the world.

From a college student who didn't click the privacy box: "Cisco just offered me a job! Now I have to weigh the utility of a fatty paycheck against the daily commute to San Jose and hating work."

From a social media strategist on Chrysler's corporate Twitter account: "I find it ironic that Detroit is known as the #motorcity and yet no one here knows how to f***ing drive."

From a White House aide about to be fired: "Growing problem for the Administration—too many 1st term holdovers not getting the hint that it's time to move on and get the f*** out."

From a food truck employee about to get fired: "Shout out to the good people of Glass, Lewis & Co. for placing a $170 order and not leaving a tip."

From a firefighter about to get fired for sexist comments: "Reject a woman and she will never let it go. One of the many defects of their kind. Also weak arms."

From a California Pizza Kitchen employee about to get fired over his tweet about new uniforms: "@calpizzakitchen black button ups are the lamest s*** ever!!! #CaliporniaSkeetzaKitchen."

From a CFO: "Dinner w/Board tonite. Used to be fun. Now one must be on guard every second."

2

Look at the Stars

Don't confuse fame with success.
Madonna is one; Helen Keller is the other.

—Erma Bombeck

Justin Bieber made the cover of *Forbes* while still a teenager, earned $58 million in the year that followed, and pulled in more Twitter followers than Barack Obama. He also was recorded peeing into a mop bucket while leaving a nightclub, shouting profanity at a photo of former President Clinton, and spitting over a balcony. Then he got a DUI arrest and, according to CNN, allegedly smoked pot with his father on a chartered flight. Here's his answer when asked about people who criticize his behavior: "I don't give a f***."

By the time he turned 20, Justin Bieber had become the poster boy for a pop culture that affects nearly every aspect of how we live and work.

Celebrities today treat us to their self-posted "nip slips," digital feuds, and Twitter updates on their sex lives. Kanye West interrupts Taylor Swift's acceptance speech at the 2009 MTV Video Music Awards to let the world know he thinks she should not have won and then later credits his own "fight for justice" for the attention that followed. In the air, celebrities shove flight attendants, turn over snack carts, and pound on walls. In hotels, they throw furniture, burn carpets, and do thousands of dollars of damage. In their family lives, many have moved well beyond the simple affair to sex addiction, domestic violence, and even sexual assault. In some cases, their careers barely suffer. Singer Chris Brown combined multiple assault arrests with behavior such as tossing chairs at TV studio windows and screaming at parking lot attendants—while still producing albums.

Athletes are just as bad as entertainers. An Oklahoma State guard shoves a fan during a college basketball game. A tennis star curses out a lineswoman. A major-league pitcher posts a photo of himself giving the middle finger. Too many players get arrested, and, in some sports, fans can almost assume that the top athletes are using performance-enhancing drugs. It's not just that athletes are no longer heroes. In his book *Something Like the Gods: A Cultural History of the Athlete from Achilles to LeBron,* author Stephen Amidon goes so far as to suggest that fans today often don't even like the athletes they cheer but rather see them as "a target for their frustrations with a disenchanting world." Sports stars have become people we love to hate.

IT WASN'T ALWAYS LIKE THIS

Celebrities behaving badly is nothing new, but the public didn't always shrug it off. When pop singer Eddie Fisher divorced actress Debbie Reynolds in 1959 to marry Elizabeth Taylor, his career suffered badly and his NBC television show was canceled. Knowing that misbehavior would carry consequences, the entertainment industry covered it up. Actor Robert J. Wagner wrote in his memoir that a drunk- driving arrest in Old Hollywood would lead to "a nod, a wink, perhaps some modest amount of money changing hands, and that would be the end of it." He added, "If an actor behaved the way that, say, Tiger Woods did—and believe me, it was not unusual—it was covered up."

Today, the kind of thing that used to end a career now makes it. Kim Kardashian became a household name by making a sex tape, and Miley Cyrus set a record for generating the most tweets per minute when she twerked on the 2013 MTV Video Music Awards broadcast—just weeks before releasing a chart-topping single. In her book *Celebrity, Inc.: How Famous People Make Money*, author Jo Piazza notes that of the 16 mistresses alleged to have been involved in the Tiger Woods 2010 scandal, four appeared in *Vanity Fair*, three competed on Howard Stern's radio show for the crown of Miss Mistress and a prize of $100,000, one wrote a tell-all book, one starred in a pornographic movie, and one became a correspondent for the entertainment news show *Extra*.

With this kind of power and money, celebrity shapes our culture in many ways. Plastic surgery is on the rise, even in young people, now that social media makes it easier than ever to compare your own selfies with what celebrities post. A free app even lets girls and women take a selfie and then tinker with their face, hair, and makeup before comparing the original photo with the "improved" one.

Celebrity has become big business, generating billions of dollars annually, and that may be a factor in the entitlement that grows as celebrities travel all over the place, make more and more money, and lose all sense of decorum. Companies spend more than $50 billion on celebrity endorsements, and about 15 percent of U.S. advertisements now feature celebrities. Singer Beyoncé reportedly signed a multiyear endorsement deal with Pepsi for $50 million, and soccer star David Beckham reportedly earns $55,000 per day just for his celebrity endorsements. A Nielsen study found that

64 percent of American adults who follow a celebrity online also follow a brand and that a celebrity follower is four times more likely to follow a brand than the average U.S. adult online. A separate 2011 study found that athlete endorsements generated a 4 percent revenue growth in the endorsed brands. College sports are big business, too. The NCAA reportedly ran a $71-million surplus in 2012, and Big Ten schools raked in $315 million for sports events in 2012 alone.

Athletes may make an even bigger impact than entertainers. According to Amidon, "Rappers, rockers, movie stars, politicians, self-help gurus, and talk show hosts all have their constituencies, but none of them have the ability to stop the world in its tracks like the athlete."

Fans seem to take their cue from the worst of what they see in their idols. Think of the Cleveland Indians baseball fans who chanted "Detroit's bankrupt" during a 2013 game against the Detroit Tigers. Or the adult baseball fan who barreled over a child while trying to retrieve a home run ball. Or the crowd that cheers an opposing player's injury. This kind of behavior has made its way to youth sports fields, where kids now deal with Little League Parent Syndrome, named for adults who engage in verbal— and, occasionally, physical—abuse.

More troubling is the possibility that a whole range of serious social problems could be linked to sports celebrity. In their book *When Winning Costs Too Much: Steroids, Supplements, and Scandal in Today's Sports World,* John Bailes and John McCloskey say that sports contributes to social problems including violence, academic fraud, and authority figures abusing their positions to seek self-satisfaction instead of setting honorable examples. A 2012 study finds that about one in 20 teens has used steroids to increase muscle mass.

In entertainment and in sports, role models are getting harder to find. Kim Kardashian and Honey Boo Boo probably generate more revenue than more artistically accomplished stars of the small screen, but becoming a role model should be about offering something more. I know moms who no longer let their daughters watch Hannah Montana because they aren't prepared to answer questions about Miley Cyrus today.

Basketball bad boy Charles Barkley once said, "I'm not paid to be a role model." I disagree, especially since he said it in a TV commercial for Nike, which markets sneakers to teens. Stars have to know that millions of people are watching them, including kids who may not have role models at home. There has to be some decorum in how you present yourself, and that's especially true if you're going to be in the public eye. When you sell your personal reputation for an endorsement deal, your private life no longer belongs just to you. And when you drag your family through whatever personal mess you make, the public can and should hold you accountable for the environment you're creating for the children you're raising. Tiger Woods may be the world's greatest golfer, and I personally don't care how many women he sleeps with, but I do care that he hurt his wife and children. Amidon explains that plenty of people cheat on their wives, that Tiger had great success despite racism, and that none of that mattered when his scandal broke: "By getting his jollies with cocktail waitresses, Woods had betrayed a public that had been taught that the ability to hit a three iron to within inches of a cup while millions watched translated into personal qualities like honesty and unadulterated devotion."

The sports and entertainment stars who behave outrageously dominate the culture in a way that makes it all too easy to forget that a higher standard is possible. That leaves us with one major resource for change: ourselves.

PUT VALUES INTO ACTION

One by one, individuals and businesses can change the culture by choosing and acting on a clear set of values. Here are steps to help make that happen and make some money along the way.

1. *Know What You Stand For*: Decide what you want your enterprise to be known for and stick with it. Marilyn Monroe could have been speaking for any number of modern-day celebrities when she said, "It's better for the whole world to know you, even as a sex star, than never to be known at all." But even though she made herself one of the biggest stars in the world, she never quite succeeded in her goal of proving herself as a serious actress. In the business arena, a company such as GoDaddy can get national attention with marketing filled with sexual innuendo, only to find that potential customers don't know what it does. Whatever your business priorities are, make sure that they are clear and consistent.

2. *Set Clear Expectations*: Identify the important values that represent the core of the organization, and then translate those values into clear standards for employees at different levels, so that the workforce understands what it looks like to live the values.

3. *Hire Based on Business Values*: Resist the temptation to overemphasize presentation skills at the expense of candidates with a track record of real achievement. The more clearly you understand and communicate your business priorities, the more likely you'll be to bring in talent that will strengthen your culture and boost your bottom line.

4. *Turn Corporate Role Models into Mentors*: Take the time to identify the people in your organization who are doing the best job of putting corporate values into action. These people are likely to be major internal influencers even if they're not the ones most frequently putting their names forward for recognition. Train these people as mentors who can build internal alignment.

5. *Hold Your Team Accountable*: Know when to give second chances. I believe in giving second chances to valued team members who have made

an isolated mistake that is not illegal and not unethical, as long as they take responsibility and also understand that apologizing isn't enough; they must know the mistake cannot be repeated. But if a mistake is repeated, maybe that person doesn't get a third chance to do damage to company values.

6. *Have the Hard Conversations*: Part of holding a team accountable is having tough conversations. I learned a lot about having hard conversations when I took over as president of a professional association with 1,750 members and I discovered the challenge of managing high-powered volunteers who know they can't be fired. When someone misses the mark, the only option is to sit down and talk openly about the situation, even if the conversation leads to an organizational change. What helps me is to remember to focus on the issue and not the person. Generally, I find that the less lousy you make someone feel, the better the outcome is. I'm not perfect, and I'm not always as careful as I'd like to be, but it does help that people know I genuinely care about them. I still remember what it was like to start out as a young buyer in the fashion industry and have a manager berate me publicly for a $3-million problem I inherited, and I make sure that my team gets treated better. When a new team member misses the mark while learning our company standards, we sit that person down to review the facts, lay out the consequences of any future errors, and share a path for development based on expected improvements. The error can be something as simple as missing an after-hours conference call. What matters is the principle. You the employee are not bad, but we the company don't accept "my bad."

7. *Know When to Pass the Ball*: No one excels at everything. In sports, entertainment, and business, success requires knowing where you're weak as well as where you excel. Outside the athletic arena, figuring out those areas can be a challenge. If you've been an *American Idol* fan, you've probably

23

noticed that some of the worst auditions come from contestants who truly believe they're the next big thing. As it turns out, research on "the *American Idol* effect" shows that people in general are not the best judges of their own creativity. Understand where you need help, and set an example for requesting it humbly.

8. *Adapt to Change*: While your values remain constant, you'll need to change the way your business operates in the marketplace. For example, you may need to rethink how you recruit as a new generation of employees changes jobs more frequently and virtual employees, part-time employees, and independent contractors become more common. The old hiring mind-set said you should hire only up-and-coming superstars. Today it's better to consider all the hiring possibilities: experienced retirees who may want to reengage, alumni who previously left your company, stay-at-home parents reentering the workforce, skilled employees who live in another location and work virtually, or contractors who can give you quick access to skills not available internally. Your next great hire may live on the other side of the world or right next door.

9. *Be Yourself Consistently*: Business school professors Rob Goffee and Gareth Jones conducted research on the relationship between authenticity and effective leadership and found that people simply will not follow a leader they feel is inauthentic. And executives made it clear that to be authentic, they needed to work for an authentic organization.

10. *Balance Authenticity with Boundaries*: You probably spend more time with your colleagues than your family, and you may naturally build close personal ties. Of course, you need to let your team know whether a personal matter may affect your work schedule, and, if you're fortunate to work in a supportive environment, your colleagues will want to do everything they can to support you. If you're a manager, sharing personal information can also help build a team spirit by making you more human and relatable. But be aware of the dangers of oversharing. I've known of executives who use business relationships to share everything from details about romantic encounters to specifics about their gastric distress.

THE PAYOFF

The commitment to act on business values starts at the top, and that puts disproportionate pressure on executive leadership. But companies that unite their workforce behind clear priorities have the best chance of succeeding as the pace of change increases. While I'm working on the person in the mirror, I'll also remind myself of the people in the public eye with qualities I do admire, such as the work ethic and dignity of Arnold Palmer or the grace and talent of Meryl Streep or the tenacity of Bonnie St. John, the first African American to win medals in winter Paralympic competition as a ski racer. St. John's right leg was amputated below the knee when she was five. When she placed second in her 1984 race, here's what she said: "I was ahead in the slalom, but in the second run, everyone fell on a dangerous spot. I was beaten by a woman who got up faster than I did. I learned that people fall down, winners get up, and gold medal winners just get up faster." Her words and her achievement have helped me do better in my own life as a boss, a mentor, a wife, a mother, a daughter, and a contributor to the community.

And I'll think of all the millions of noncelebrities who, if we all made an effort to set an example, could quickly overshadow the misbehavior featured in the media and inspire each other the way the stars used to inspire us. Who knows—maybe one day some of our fallen stars will consider changing their ways to be worthy of us.

CAUGHT!
HOW STARS SAY "MY BAD"

"I is what I is, and I'm not changing!" —cookbook author Paula Deen suggesting that she doesn't need to change when it comes to using racial slurs

"I don't know why the girl had me say those things." —LA Clippers owner Donald Sterling, explaining his racist remarks

"I just snapped and reacted and did what many athletes have done and paid the price for it." —boxer Mike Tyson on why he bit Evander Holyfield's ear

"I meant to say 'maggot' but I have a lisp." —actor Charlie Sheen after getting caught using a homophobic slur

"My father and I used to do this all the time, y'all!" —pop singer Britney Spears on driving with a child in her lap and not in a car seat

"I think what happens is you're, at the time, you're betting football and then, then what's after football is basketball . . . and obviously the next thing that follows is baseball. It's just a pattern that you got into." —former baseball player and manager Pete Rose admitting that he bet on baseball after 15 years of denials

"I didn't have the tools to know how to do it the right way, how to let go the right way. I'd never been taught that." —country singer LeAnn Rimes on why she started an affair with her second husband before ending her first marriage

"My actions were out of frustration during the heat of the game, period." —pro basketball player Kobe Bryant after getting caught hurling a gay slur at a referee

"Although Alec acknowledges that he should have used different language in parenting his child, everyone who knows him privately knows what he has been put through for the past six years." —a spokesperson for actor Alec Baldwin implying that the actor's ex-wife was to blame when he called his daughter a "thoughtless pig"

"I generally tend to speak before thinking, which is something I wish I could change about myself. But it has been 41 years now and I don't really see that happening." —reality TV star Brandi Glanville on why she made a racial joke about a costar

"Personal sins should not require press releases, and problems within a family shouldn't have to mean public confessions." —golfer Tiger Woods following the car accident that led to the exposure of his infidelities

"No." —Lance Armstrong on whether he thought using performance-enhancing drugs was cheating

3

The One Bipartisan Effort

The road to power is paved with hypocrisy and casualties. Never regret.

—Frank Underwood, fictional politician featured
on the Netflix show House of Cards

No one chokes on an apology like a politician. At best, "my bad" takes the form of something like "I misspoke" or "Mistakes were made" or "I deeply regret any instance in which anyone was foolish enough to take offense at my innocent actions." But the political nonapology typically comes only after other options have failed. With ethical lapses commonplace and broken promises expected, the nonapology serves as the exclamation point on a statement of broken trust.

DENIAL (NOT THE RIVER IN EGYPT)

When I was 14 and my parents caught me sneaking out of the house to go out with friends, I saw no choice but to apologize and accept the consequences: I was grounded for a month, less than ideal, while I regained my parents' trust. I was humiliated, upset that I upset my parents, and, worse, disappointed that I had to forgo activities that my friends were doing. I learned the lessons of consequences at a very early age. That's how it works for most people. Not for politicians. When caught red-handed, politicians take their first cue from the Marx brothers with a response that seems to say, "Who are you gonna believe, me or your own eyes?" No evidence is strong enough to squash a politician's impulse to deny. It doesn't matter whether they've just tweeted a picture of their privates to an account with thousands of followers, or gotten caught with a freezer full of bribe money, or solicited an undercover cop for sex in an airport restroom. First comes the denial.

In fact, when most of us would want to recoil in the face of incriminating evidence, politicians only deny louder. Case in point: Illinois Governor Rod Blagojevich. Blagojevich was caught on tape attempting to auction off the senate seat left vacant by Barack Obama. The FBI taped him saying things such as this gem: "I've got this thing and it's f***ing golden, and, uh, uh, I'm just not giving it up for f***-in' nothing. I'm not gonna do it. And, and I can always use it. I can parachute me there." Blagojevich didn't just deny. He launched a national media blitz proclaiming his innocence with appearances on shows such as *The View*, *The Daily Show*, *Late Show with David Letterman*, and even *Celebrity Apprentice*.

ANYTHING BUT STRAIGHT TALK

When denial isn't quite enough, politicians turn to stonewalling tactics from cover-ups to misleading statements to sudden memory loss. There is seemingly no limit to the number of times a tarnished politician will lose the ability to recall any detail surrounding any action that could in any way be relevant to an allegation of misbehavior. This is especially the case with scandals involving high-level politicians. Scott J. Basinger of the University of Houston studied presidential scandals between 1972 and 2008 and, in research published in *Political Science Quarterly* and titled "Skeletons in White House Closets: A Discussion of Modern Presidential Scandals," concluded that the White House is significantly more likely to stonewall when allegations involve the president.

"A serious question like that deserves more than the lies my opponent is offering. Lies, I remind you, that he stole from MY campaign!"

More puzzling is how often politicians show an instinct for embellishments that add to their troubles or even create problems where none existed. It's hard to imagine what Bill Clinton hoped to gain when he said he smoked marijuana but "didn't inhale." He might have just stopped after "smoked marijuana." Or what vice presidential candidate Paul Ryan was thinking when he shaved more than an hour off his marathon time in a media interview, as if no one would check on an assertion that according to runnersworld.com would have made him one of the top 2 percent of marathon finishers in 2011.

Under pressure, politicians see no hair too small to split. Connecticut Senate candidate Richard Blumenthal blamed a prepositional slip of the tongue when he was caught having repeatedly said that he had served in Vietnam—even though he'd actually received five military deferments before enlisting in the Marine Reserve, enabling him to avoid combat overseas. So he went on the attack. "On a few occasions I have misspoken about my service, and I regret that and I take full responsibility," Blumenthal said. "But I will not allow anyone to take a few misplaced words and impugn my record of service to our country."

Attacking critics is one way that scandal-tinged politicians position themselves as victims. Rod Blagojevich used some classic moves when he compared his arrest to the attack on Pearl Harbor. He told the Associated Press about the day of his arrest, "Dec. 9 to my family, to us, to me, is what Pearl Harbor Day was to the United States." He built on the theme when he told NBC that as the day unfolded, "I thought about Mandela, Dr. King, and Gandhi and tried to put some perspective to all this and that is what I am doing now." Other politicians who have fought scandal by comparing themselves to Nelson Mandela include Bill Clinton and Anthony Weiner. San Diego Mayor Bob Filner compared his situation to facing a lynch mob when he resigned under a barrage of sexual harassment complaints from more than a dozen women.

South Carolina Governor Mark Sanford compared himself to the biblical figure King David as a way to explain why he would not resign after he was caught abandoning his post to rendezvous with his mistress in Argentina. He was resisting calls for resignation not because he wished to minimize the consequences of his wrongdoing but because he was inspired by David, "who after his fall from grace humbly refocused on the work at hand." When Sanford subsequently ran for Congress and faced both political attacks and legal action for violating his divorce agreement, he took out an ad comparing himself to Commander William Travis at the Alamo.

NONAPOLOGIZE

The political rule of thumb seems to be this: when all else fails, nonapologize. I've been following politics since I was a teenager, especially as a political science major in college, and I can't remember ever hearing a sincere apology from a politician. Instead, we get whopping nonapologies, starting with the classic "Mistakes were made." Presidential administrations of both parties going back to Ulysses Grant have been using that approach, according to William Safire in *Safire's Political Dictionary*. Political figures find all kinds of ways around making a full apology. Newt Gingrich suggested that patriotism made him do it when he explained his marital infidelities as the presidential race approached: "There's no question at times of my life, partially driven by how passionately I felt about this country, that I worked far too hard and things happened in my life that were not appropriate." On *60 Minutes* Arnold Schwarzenegger used "I'm not perfect" as a way to explain how he could father a child with his housekeeper during his marriage. Not perfect? And if you think an apology at the very least means admitting to doing *something* wrong, consider this classic from Bob Packwood, who resigned from the Senate after his own diary, subpoenaed by the Senate Ethics Committee, incriminated him on sexual harassment allegations: "I'm apologizing for the conduct that it was alleged that I did."

DEMAND REDEMPTION

The apparent goal: hit the career reset button as quickly as possible by any means possible. In the old days, politicians might have spent years rehabilitating themselves before reentering the public arena. These days the waiting period seems to be two years, tops. Two years was the waiting time not only for Anthony Weiner but also for Mark Sanford, who ran for congressional office postscandal with a campaign that highlighted a "God of second chances." Eliot Spitzer spent just eight and a half months in seclusion before returning to public life, according to *The New York Times.* New York City Rep. Charles Rangel hung on to his seat after a House ethics panel convicted him of 11 counts of violating ethics rules, including some significant tax violations, and then he blamed *the American people* for the low approval ratings of Congress. On the MSNBC show *Jansing and Co.*, he said of the approval ratings, "It's totally embarrassing, but worse than the Congress is the silence of people that could make a difference." Scandal-tarred politicians who don't campaign still often do just fine: Bob Packwood moved to a successful lobbying career as did Larry Craig, the former senator who left office following an incident with an undercover cop in an airport bathroom.

THE ULTIMATE COMEBACK

Of course, no modern politician has come back from scandal like Bill Clinton, and Clinton's rebound from Monicagate hints at the potential benefits of a genuine apology. After making seriously misleading statements under oath as president, Clinton not only survived impeachment but also left office with high approval ratings and a reputation that has grown so much that he now ranks tops in forgiveability among some famous public figures who have lied. A *60 Minutes/Vanity Fair* poll released in 2014 showed that more Americans are willing to forgive Bill Clinton than a variety of other public figures who have lied, including Lance Armstrong, Richard Nixon, and Bernie Madoff, who ranked last.

The key to Clinton's recovery may have been his eventual willingness to show contrition, even if for many it was too little, too late. In the book *Political Tone: How Leaders Talk and Why*, authors Roderick P. Hart, Jay P. Childers, and Colene J. Lind argue that Clinton learned from and improved on the initial petulance marked by his famous finger wag. He later changed his tone with lines such as this: "I'm having to become quite an expert in this business of asking for forgiveness." And this: "Like anyone who honestly faces the shame of wrongful conduct, I would give anything to go back and undo what I did." He stayed away from denial words, and he avoided going negative. And at least some forgave him; as of 2014, 43 percent of Americans were willing to forgive him, according to the *60 Minutes/Vanity Fair* poll.

I interpret this story as confirmation of my belief that an apology can work wonders when it comes across as sincere and humble, and I believe that the best way to come across that way is to be sincere and humble. I also believe that Clinton's legacy would be brighter if he had started with a humble apology or, better yet, avoided the trouble in the first place. No matter what else he did while in office, the first thing many people of my generation will remember about him is the punch line, "I did not have sexual relations with that woman."

Others may take a different view. In 2013, a defiant Lance Armstrong told *Texas Monthly* that Bill Clinton is "a hero of mine" who proves that "ultimately, people forgive and forget and remember the good stuff you did."

THE PUBLIC VIEW: LOWER THAN LICE

For better or worse, avoiding a true apology has helped politicians whose first goal is to continue a political career. In a study published in *Political Research Quarterly* and titled "Scandals and Congressional Elections in the Post-Watergate Era," political scientist Scott J. Basinger found that while incumbents tarnished by scandal were far more likely to retire or resign, nearly three-quarters of those who decided to run again survived their primaries and 81 percent of those who made it to the general election kept their seats.

But keeping the career comes at the cost of public trust. According to a 2013 poll from Public Policy Polling, people have a lower opinion of Congress than they do of root canals, NFL replacement refs, head lice, the rock band Nickelback, colonoscopies, Washington, DC, political pundits, carnies, traffic jams, cockroaches, Donald Trump, France, Genghis Khan, and used-car salespeople. When your profession becomes the butt of late-night comics, maybe the time has come to rethink business as usual. Unfortunately, the only people willing to run for office these days are the ones who perpetuate the status quo. By giving endless second chances to misbehaving politicians who show little or no remorse, voters wind up with political leaders who act like the worst celebrity divas but with the power to screw things up in a big way. To paraphrase H.L. Mencken, if we're getting the democracy we deserve, we are indeed getting it good and hard.

SHOW INTEGRITY

Modern politicians have sucked the trust out of the culture more than any other professional class. Here are some simple steps that business executives can use to reverse the trend by standing for integrity.

1. *Walk Your Talk*: One reason no one trusts politicians is that so few pay any significant attention to campaign promises once they're in office. The simple act of keeping your word can do more to inspire trust and meaningful action than any message-tested speech.

2. *Get the Easy Things Right*: With so much of the business world operating in shades of gray, most leaders face a complex ethical dilemma at some point. In the meantime, make a statement for integrity by getting the hundreds of easy things right, from submitting accurate expense reports to resisting the temptation to cap scores at a triple bogey when you're golfing with clients.

3. *Meet Deadlines*: Every time you meet a deadline, you build trust that you're one of those rare people who keeps their word. If you can't meet a deadline, say so up front and have that hard conversation before disappointment builds. If you miss a deadline, apologize and keep the schedules going forward.

4. *Be the Same Person with Everyone*: An old truism says you can learn a lot about someone by how he or she treats a waiter. The receptionist, the janitor, the postal carrier, and the board chair all should know you as the same person.

5. *Try Transparency*: Business school professors Rob Goffee and Gareth Jones advocate for "radical honesty" based on the idea that secrets are almost impossible to keep in the age of Facebook, WikiLeaks, and Twitter. I learned a similar principle from my father, a corporate executive who told me that people at the top have the least stress because they know what's going on. That stuck with me, and so I work to empower the JBK team with knowledge by providing weekly updates on business goals and challenges. It's not easy to do without spin in business or politics. When I watch proceedings on political scandals, I can't help but think of all the senior executive job candidates who tell my team that they can't recall key facts about their own backgrounds, from their academic performance to their base compensation. I would understand if people said they'd rather not discuss their GPA because that represents a different time in their life. I can also understand not knowing exactly what your stock options are worth at any given time, but who just forgets their salary? And do they really think we won't investigate if we sense they've misled us? I've seen senior executives misstate their income by $75,000. If you don't want to share something, say so. If you do, tell the truth.

6. *Use Plain Words*: The moment you start using words such as "transitioning," "rightsizing," and "corporate redesign," you remind employees of all the times that similar words have been used to cast people from jobs as a way to limit costs. As much as possible, use clear words so that your team knows what to expect.

7. *Share Credit*: Sharing credit is another trust builder that strengthens teamwork. It's always a red flag for my team when a candidate for a senior position comes to our office and fills an interview with all "I" and no "we." Unfortunately, this mind-set has become increasingly common, as research shows that Americans are becoming more narcissistic. But top businesses today are seeking people who collaborate, and more executives could take their cue from the practice of former President George H.W. Bush, who asked his speechwriters to revise remarks with what they called "I-ectomies."

8. *Do Something for Someone Else*: Even better, rebel against the current political and business climate and do something for someone else *quietly*. No one but you may ever know that you've taken a few moments to help someone anonymously, but knowing will affect how you carry yourself for the rest of the day.

9. *Hold Yourself Accountable*: The day you start a job, you own its problems. Resist the temptation to act like a political leader who seems to answer every question by blaming the last administration. Whether you or your predecessor or your team has messed up, you may need to apologize. Not too long ago my firm submitted work with an error that made its way to a senior client executive. Within two hours of discovering the error, my vice president had fixed it and apologized and I had sent my own note of apology saying that we made a mistake, that the mistake was our fault, that it should not have happened, and that it will not happen again. I've worked in places where staffers might just shrug off client annoyance as an honest error, but we value our client relationships and are committed to holding ourselves accountable.

10. *Fail Well*: When people ask me how to become successful in their careers, the first thing I tell them is to keep going no matter what. I learned resilience as a child at a summer camp that rewarded achievement by handing out feathers and where I failed in my quest to earn the coveted fuchsia feather for "Girl of the Week." That elusive feather was my first experience with rejection, and learning how to keep going has helped me more as an entrepreneur than all the awards I've since won combined. While I may not always meet my own standards, I've tried to set an example for my team on how to handle setbacks with grace. The last recession in particular tested me, and some days it was all I could do to take care of my health and start each day with my own version of a personal pep talk, which often went something like this: "Yesterday stunk; let's see what today brings." It helped me build positive energy, and our business survived and came out of the recession stronger than ever. In a culture that encourages the losing team to blame the refs, you can stand out by failing well. Hold your head high, keep going, and show those around you that you mean it when you say, "We'll get 'em next time."

THE PAYOFF

Every organization has slipups, but businesses don't have to choose between doing right and doing well. If it's tackled head-on, an ethical slip can even have benefits. One study from the University of Central Florida shows that if a company responds vigorously to a breach in ethics, employees who witnessed the breach end up more satisfied than if no failure had occurred at all. I believe that's a reflection of the power of showing a team that you're willing to do hard things to keep a commitment. Every person willing to make this effort can help counter the prevailing political culture, and any business executives who show that they're smart and informed as well as ethical certainly would have my serious consideration as a voter should they run for public office.

"MY BAD" TAKES OFFICE

When "my bad" goes to Washington or the state capitol, apologies sound like almost anything except what you want to hear: "I'm sorry for what I did wrong. It's my fault. It won't happen again." Here's the kind of thing that comes out instead:

"It was a misstatement; I misspoke . . . I've said something that is similar to that but quite acceptable for a long time." —presidential candidate nominee Mitt Romney explaining why he said "I'm not concerned about the very poor"

"There is a line between routine politics, political horse-trading, campaign fund-raising, official acts, and how you ask for political funds. It was always my intention in all the things I discussed back in 2008 to try to see if I could do those things on the right side of the line. I thought they were permissible." —former Gov. Rod Blagojevich following his conviction on corruption charges for which he was sentenced to 14 years in prison

"Mistakes were clearly made, and as a result we let down the people we're entrusted to serve." —Gov. Chris Christie on his administration's involvement in the politically motivated closing of the George Washington Bridge

"I used a term that was commonly used during my days growing up on a farm in central California. I know that this term is not used in the same way nowadays, and I meant no disrespect." —Rep. Don Young on why he used a racial slur to describe Latinos

"I deeply apologize for how people have taken the statement." —Rep. Joe Salazar on suggesting that women on college campuses shouldn't be trusted to protect themselves with firearms because they might fire carelessly upon feeling threatened

THE POLITICAL INSULT

Watching the pundits on MSNBC and Fox go at it, listening to candidates lament the "politics of insult," you might think that personal insults are a modern phenomenon. In actuality, civility in the political arena has long been in short supply. A sampling from history:

"That dark designing sordid ambitious vain proud arrogant and vindictive knave."—Charles Lee on George Washington, according to *The Lee Papers*, 1754–1811, Charles Lee, Sir Henry Bunbury

A "hideous hermaphroditical character which has neither the force and firmness of a man, nor the gentleness and sensibility of a woman." —description of John Adams by supporters of Thomas Jefferson in the presidential election of 1800, according to PBS *American Experience*

A "mean-spirited, low-lived fellow, the son of a half-breed Indian squaw, sired by a Virginia mulatto father." —description of Thomas Jefferson in a leaflet by Adams's team in the presidential election of 1800, according to PBS *American Experience*

"Like a rotten mackerel in the moonlight, he both shines and stinks." —Virginia aristocrat John Randolph in the 1820s on Henry Clay, according to *The New York Times* article "The Paradox of Corrupt Yet Effective Leadership"

"Despot," "Buffoon," "Old Scoundrel," and "Ignoramus Abe." — names flung at Abraham Lincoln during the election of 1860, according to Rosemarie Ostler, author of *Slinging Mud: Rude Nicknames, Scurrilous Slogans, and Insulting Slang from Two Centuries of American Politics*

A "cold-blooded, narrow-minded, prejudiced, obstinate, timid old psalm-singing Indianapolis politician." —Theodore Roosevelt on President Benjamin Harrison in 1889, according to Rich Rubino, author of *The Political Bible of Little Known Facts in American Politics*

"A no good lying bastard." —former President Truman on Richard Nixon when Nixon sought the presidency in 1960, according to Rubino

"Poor George, he can't help it. He was born with a silver foot in his mouth." —Democratic Texas Governor Ann Richards speaking about Republican presidential nominee George H.W. Bush at the 1988 Democratic National Convention

THE STATE OF TRUST

A survey conducted by the Pew Research Center in 2013 put trust in government near record lows: only 19 percent of Americans said that they trust the government in Washington to do what is right just about always or most of the time.

When the Pew National Election Study first asked this question in 1958, 73 percent of Americans trusted the government to do what is right just about always or most of the time.

Worldwide, government saw the largest decline in trust of any institution in 2014, and the largest drop in trust in government was seen in the United States (plummeting 16 points to 37 percent), France (17 points to 32 percent), and Hong Kong (18 points to 45 percent), according to the 2014 Edelman Trust Barometer.

Illinois residents trust their state government to handle their state's problems far less than residents in any other state, according to a 2014 Gallup survey. Gallup calls the state's low rank not surprising, given that the state's past two governors were sentenced to jail for crimes committed while in office.

CEOs and government leaders rank at the bottom of the list of trusted sources of information about companies, according to the 2014 Edelman Trust Barometer. Academics and experts top the list.

Twenty-four percent of American employees don't trust their employer, according to the American Psychological Association's 2014 Work and Well-Being Survey.

More than 80 percent of those surveyed believe that being effective in their work requires a high degree of trust in their leaders, according to Building Trust 2013: Workforce Trends Defining High Performance, a survey of more than 290 organizations conducted by Interaction Associates in partnership with the Human Capital Institute.

Low-performing organizations, those whose net profit grew less than 5 percent or shrank over the previous year, are significantly more likely to try to increase profits by reducing costs, improving efficiency, and increasing productivity, while high-performing organizations, those whose net profit grew more than 5 percent over the previous year, focus on customer loyalty to build the top line, according to the Building Trust 2013 survey.

4

At Your Service . . . Or Not

To put it into perspective, 3,000 passengers were impacted by the Triumph incident. None was hurt. It was a passenger comfort issue. We apologized.

—Carnival Corporation former-CEO Micky Arison in 2013 about an incident that left cruise passengers adrift for days without working toilets

My cable company can get away with sloppy service because it has me trapped, but few businesses enjoy this luxury today. The sorry state of customer service in service-related businesses shows the pitfalls of acting like a commodity business in a service economy.

I once thought it would be fun to take a cruise. We set sail from California and headed to Catalina and then onto Ensenada, Mexico, where passengers started getting sick. As the ship made its way toward Mexico, more and more people fell ill with severe GI symptoms. By the time the cruise liner returned to port, on day three of what was supposed to be a four-day journey, more than 600 passengers and crew members had contracted shigellosis, a virulent intestinal illness. One got sick with intestinal symptoms and died of an apparent heart attack in a hospital in Ensenada. At some point, I decided not to cruise again.

My personal cruise from hell isn't as unusual as I had hoped. In the first 13 weeks of 2014, epidemics of gastrointestinal illness broke out on eight cruise ships, according to CDC data. Illness is just one of the serious potential problems that cruise passengers face. According to Senate testimony by cruise industry authority Ross A. Klein, in 2013 alone the media reported the following about cruise ships: three running aground; five fires; two collisions; 19 mechanical problems including power loss, propulsion problems, and generator problems; 10 canceled port calls and/or changes in itinerary; 16 cruises with delayed embarkation and/or disembarkation; two cruises where passengers were bumped; and eight ships that failed U.S. health inspections.

Cruise lines don't seem worried. During an infamous 2013 cruise, as passengers aboard the Carnival *Triumph* drifted in the Gulf of Mexico without electricity or working toilets on a ship where they reported urine-soaked floors and walls seeping raw sewage, Carnival Corp. CEO Micky Arison sat courtside at a Miami Heat basketball game. He later explained to the *Wall Street Journal* that the onboard conditions caused by an engine room fire were a "passenger comfort issue" leaving no one "hurt."

Something is wrong when the world's largest vacation company, the one that for years marketed itself on "fun," can traumatize and endanger thousands of customers and then shrug off the problem as a "comfort issue." In too many service businesses, "my bad" has started to sound like "Hey, at least we didn't kill anyone."

Consider these facts from the travel and hospitality industry:

- Nearly one in five cruise passengers has a problem on their cruise, according to the 2013 J.D. Power 2013 Cruise Line Satisfaction Report.
- Customer experience in the hotel industry took a nosedive in 2014 with a decrease that marked the largest change in any industry's average rating, according to a ranking by the customer experience research and consulting firm Temkin Group.
- Americans rank airlines lower on customer service than any industry except cable TV, social networks, and Internet service providers, according to the 2014 American Customer Satisfaction Index.

Clearly, I'm not the only one who's noticed that travel used to be more fun. The numbers-first/customer-last approach has created a world in which cruise passengers now feel grateful if their vacation doesn't sicken them, hotel guests routinely share quarters with bedbugs, and airline passengers expect to do battle to redeem the miles they've "earned." In one extreme case, an airline denied a dying veteran a refund on a ticket purchased before he knew he was terminal, a decision ultimately reversed under public pressure.

Without a service focus, businesses have a harder time hanging on to customers. The cruise industry's reputation has sunk below even that of commercial air travel, according to a 2014 Harris poll. And, while the airline industry has positioned itself for record profits by cutting service and adding fees, air travel has become so unappealing that many people would rather drive. Aviation consultant Mark Gerchick reports in his book *Full Upright and Locked Position: Not-So-Comfortable Truths about Air Travel Today* that, even for trips up to 500 miles, air travel dropped 17 percent between 2000 and 2010.

HELL IS A TRIP IN COACH

No wonder people will drive up to 500 miles to escape a flight. The airline industry has moved so far away from service and so far into the "my bad" mind-set that, combined with the indignities of increased security measures, flying now routinely feels inhumane. Gerchick points out that the process of catching a plane now resembles standard intake procedures at county jails: "Check identity; match government-issued ID to intake form; pat down for weapons or contraband; remove shoes, belt, jewelry, and extra clothing layers; and stand in multiple lines until directed to stand somewhere else."

It's hardly better once you board. First you fight for scarce overhead bin space, as passengers carry on everything up to and including the kitchen sink. If you're not an elite traveler who boards early, the bin over your seat may already be filled by the time you get on the plane. Then you spend hours jammed into a tiny space while hoping that the person in front of you doesn't break your laptop with a sudden move to push the seat backward. You get limited breaks for food and water provided by increasingly surly flight attendants who may respond to a simple request for juice with an attitude that makes clear what at least some of them really think of you: "We're here to save your butt—not kiss it." And, occasionally, flight attendants just lose it: in recent years media outlets have reported incidents of flight attendant behavior including throwing a coffee pot in anger; reporting to work with a loaded handgun; and, in one famous case, spewing obscenities on the PA system, pulling the emergency slide on a plane that had just landed, and using it to exit with beer can in hand.

Even if your flight arrives on time, it may take longer than it did years ago because airlines have extended scheduled arrivals to improve their on-time performance data and, in some cases, have even told pilots to fly slower to save on fuel. And if you're seated near a baby or a child who entertains himself or herself by kicking the back of your seat, the flight seems much longer still.

Fellow passengers also are behaving worse. Reports of passenger misbehavior have increased, and media outlets tell stories that would have been unthinkable years ago: a couple in first class reportedly refuses to sit down unless they are given champagne; a passenger bursts into expletives and threatens to keep kicking the back of the chair of the woman in front of him because she won't turn off her reading light; a fistfight breaks out when one man reclines his seat into the lap of another; a passenger challenges his pilot to a fight on the tarmac. The live entertainment provided by amorous couples can make the in-flight experience even more disturbing. If you're lucky, they'll use the lavatory, but that raises other issues. On the tenth anniversary of the September 11 attacks, one couple set off a security alert when they spent too long together in an airplane bathroom. Crew members alerted the captain, and a pair of fighter jets was dispatched to accompany the flight to Detroit.

MISGUIDED SERVICE CUTS

If you fly a lot today, it's hard to believe that there was ever a "Golden Age of jet travel," typically considered the 1960s and 1970s, when airlines competed on service. Travel in the good old days was elegant, service was friendly, amenities were abundant, and meals were at least hot. Even in later decades, business travel could be an escape from the daily pressures of running a home and raising a family.

But the industry's business environment changed with deregulation and increasing fuel costs, and the airlines responded with a move to capture revenue by hitting unsuspecting passengers with as many new fees as possible. Checking bags has become an extra cost with most airlines, as has changing a ticket. It's now industry standard to charge for services such as making sure you can sit next to your child or spouse on a plane. Among other fees imposed are those of up to $25 to book a flight with a human reservations agent, a $5 "passenger convenience fee" if the agent prints your boarding pass, and charges to put carry-on bags in the overhead bin—up to $50 in the case of Frontier Airlines. Ancillary fees such as these generate billions for the airlines—an estimated $42.6 billion in 2013, up from $22.6 billion in 2010.

The airlines seem to have thought of charging for everything except a trip to the bathroom, and in fact they've thought of that, too. The head of Europe's largest low-cost carrier, Ryanair CEO Michael O'Leary, said in 2009 that "one thing we have looked at is maybe putting a coin slot on the toilet door" and even offered that "if someone wanted to pay £5 to go to the toilet, I would carry them myself. I would wipe their bums for a fiver."

Airlines also have stretched employees in their search for profitability. Over the past decade, pilot salaries were reduced by as much as 40 percent at the big airlines, according to Gerchick. Flight attendants work extreme hours for a median pay that was $37,240 per year as of May 2012. Travel journalist William J. McGee, author of *Attention All Passengers: The Airlines' Dangerous Descent—and How to Reclaim Our Skies*, reports that one workforce group at American Airlines was earning 1998 wages in 2011. You can imagine the impact that all this cost cutting has on service. As one South Carolina pilot told *Reader's Digest*: "Please don't complain to me about your lost bags. My retirement was taken to help subsidize your $39 airfare."

STAND UP FOR SERVICE

The "my bad" mentality assumes that people will accept lower service as the new normal. If you believe that service matters, stand up for it. Here are 10 steps that can help.

1. *Stop Unnecessarily Ticking People Off:* In late 2013, low-cost carrier Ryanair announced a new focus on customer service in order to, as CEO Michael O'Leary put it, "stop unnecessarily pissing people off." If the CEO who suggested a "pay-to-pee" plan can recognize that customer service matters, anyone can. A lot of pitfalls are simple to avoid. I just saw this principle at work in my own life. I put some clothes in storage with a well-regarded cleaner that wasn't able to give me a receipt right away. Since another cleaner had ruined some very special pieces of clothing, I didn't feel comfortable going without a receipt. Four weeks and three phone calls later, no receipt was forthcoming, so I paid the cleaner a visit. The man who eventually spoke with me explained that the delay happened because the cleaner has to pick and choose between serving its everyday customers and serving its storage customers. Then he reassured me with these words: "We have people who gave us their stuff more than a month ago, and we still haven't taken care of it." This, to me, is a classic example of unnecessarily ticking off a customer.

2. *Fix the Small Things*: Sometimes a tiny fix is all it takes to keep a customer. At a sushi place near our office, I order sushi with brown rice, and I routinely get sushi with white rice. I'd say the restaurant gets the order wrong about 20 percent of the time, but it fixes it every single time. The people there are pleasant and fast, they try to be accommodating, and they serve a really good product. It takes them 10 minutes to fix the problem, and it's still one of my favorite places. Of course, I'll keep ordering from them.

3. *Focus on the Fundamentals*: As any golfer will tell you, when your game slides, go back to the basic fundamentals. That's true in business, too, and with the exception of businesses that have no competitors, customer service has to be fundamental. In a service business, you need to provide some sort of human interaction with people who are trained to represent your company with courtesy. You need to give customers who have a problem the chance to speak with someone who can address the problem. Think of how customer service affects you in your life. I know that when I go to the bank to pay my mortgage, I can count on a grim

interaction with service people who can hardly bear to acknowledge me. It's almost as if the bank has trained its team to make a visit so unpleasant that customers will automate every interaction—without realizing that some customers might just leave.

4. *Find Other Places to Cut*: I know how hard it is to cut when times are tough. When the hard times of 2008 and 2009 hit, I had to add half my own pay to the list of "nonessential" expenses in order to maintain the team and the quality of service that we deliver. The payoff was that we were ready when the economy shifted and we bounced back quicker than our competitors to achieve our best year ever in 2011 followed by three-year growth of 370 percent.

5. *Communicate with Customers*: You can't make a sneaky change in your product or service and expect to avoid consequences. The airline industry in particular has done a lousy job of communicating to customers about what customers are getting for what they're paying. Even though airfares have dropped dramatically since deregulation, we passengers constantly feel like we're being nickel-and-dimed—and sometimes we are. As a traveler, I'm reasonable enough to understand that service amenities cost money, but I don't like the hidden fees that have become so common. If the industry respected its customers enough to be up front about price structure changes, it might not have such a bad reputation now.

The principle applies across industries. Last year a new takeout place opened near the office, and one day the team ordered three sandwiches. Ninety minutes later, nothing had arrived. When we called, the restaurant said it was busy with a 40-sandwich order that had to be filled first. If someone had simply told us the store was backed up with a big order and would need an extra hour and a half, we would have ordered elsewhere and gone back to it another day. But when we asked why no one told us about the delay, the restaurant representative replied, "I don't like your attitude." As customers, our attitude is that we should know about circumstances that affect service. We won't go back to that restaurant.

6. *Welcome Customers like You Mean It*: I know how much a welcome means to me as a customer; in fact, that's been the determining factor in where I've bought my past few cars. As a result of my experience as a customer, I've become obsessive about how JBK employees answer the phone. Every new employee learns our phone-answering protocol and gets tested in the early weeks on the job as I call in from various outside numbers. This takes time away from other tasks, but it's worth it to me. We spent hours evaluating different options for a voice heard by callers after hours, and then we spent more hours choosing the low-key jazz music played for anyone who needs to be put on hold. If you call our office and are put on hold for more than a couple of seconds, you'll hear that a team member will be with you shortly. We want to make sure whoever calls us gets the best possible experience because, for us, the telephone welcome is a symbol of the respect we have for clients and candidates. Other companies have other symbols. GEICO Insurance does a great job of answering on a timely basis and with a nice welcome that makes you feel good that you have chosen the company to protect your car and other valuables. You may have other symbols for your own business. Think about them when you consider the welcome customers get.

7. *Call out Bad Service*: One way to oppose service shortcuts is to call them out when you see them as a customer, and social media has given travelers a more powerful way to express themselves. Take advantage to make sure providers know that bad service is not OK. *USA Today* reports that airline passengers are increasingly turning to Twitter and other social media sites to complain and resolve travel issues, noting that Twitter posts about travel rose 54 percent from 2012 to 2013. I'm a fan of the site Urbanspoon after discovering how it could have saved me heartache at a local restaurant.

My party of eight went to the restaurant on a busy night, Father's Day. We waited 15–20 minutes to order drinks, another 20 minutes to order dinner, and another hour and 20 minutes without food. The waiter had no idea what happened to the order, and the manager told us to sit down or get out, so we left and got a pizza. Had we checked social media in advance, we would have known that this restaurant had a terrible service reputation. It would have been just as simple for the manager to check on our order and keep our business; instead, he drove us away not only from his restaurant but also from others with universally negative social media reviews. Don't ever underestimate the power of word of mouth.

8. *Support Good Service*: While you're at it, if you have a good experience, say thanks. Some travel and hospitality industry executives seem to think that investing in service is unprofitable. Show them they're wrong by traveling with companies that provide you with an excellent customer experience— and share your good experiences with them. Saying thank-you certainly will set you apart: *Bloomberg Businessweek* reports that around two dozen people heaped praise on airlines in 2013, compared to the 40 who heap scorn on the airlines on an average day.

9. *Treat Customers as Humans*: A single gesture can win my loyalty as a customer. One store I do business with sent me flowers for Mother's Day. The guy who does my Internet cabling showed up in 24 hours when our office had an emergency. The people at a local Citibank branch smile when they see me. Our team talks all the time about what we can do to be extraordinary with clients, candidates, and vendors through every interaction whether in person or by e-mail, phone, text, or Skype.

10. *Recognize That You Get What You Pay For*: It's only fair to point out that when money is no object, airline passengers get plenty of service, from vintage wines and lobster thermidor to in-flight showers and, even,

with new plans announced by Etihad Airways, a miniature suite featuring a closed-off bedroom, private bathroom, and dedicated butler. On the other hand, if you fly cross-country for less than what it would cost to gas the car for the drive, you really can't complain if your checked bag doesn't fly free. Airline passenger Bill Baker learned the hard way about the service-price trade-off in 2008 when JetBlue canceled his cross-country flight and told him he was on his own if he wanted to make the trip within a day or two because the airline had kept his fare low in part by not having agreements with other airlines to help stranded passengers. Just as we need to communicate as businesses about what customers are getting for their dollar, we need to make choices as customers about where we make the trade-off between service and price.

THE PAYOFF

Businesses related to travel and hospitality can get back on track by getting back to service and in the process can inspire other industries that face upheavals. I don't think I'm the only customer who wants to be loyal. Just let me talk with a pleasant human every once in a while. Give me a heads up when something goes wrong. Fix the little stuff that you can fix. And don't keep me confined in closed quarters with 600 people battling a highly contagious intestinal illness. You'll have a customer for life.

TAKING A STAND

Some people just won't accept lousy service. These four airline travelers took action.

Posting the 20-Foot Baggage Toss: Dwayne Stewart of British Columbia forced quick action from Air Canada in 2014 when he posted a video showing baggage handlers dropping luggage into bins about 20 feet below and noted that "we all fear this is what really happens when we hand over our luggage." The YouTube clip, which got more than a million views within four days, features Stewart's explanation that his flight from Toronto was overcrowded so people volunteered to hand over carry-on luggage. While the bags are being tossed, a passenger can be heard saying, "Good thing my computer's in there." As Stewart told CBC News Toronto, "We were so shocked we had to laugh . . . It looked comical; it looked like it wasn't real." Air Canada apologized and suspended the employees involved.

Putting Protest to Song: Musician Dave Carroll posted a protest song on YouTube that chronicled his experience with United Airlines customer service after his Taylor guitar was damaged by baggage handling. Carroll says he spent nine months in a customer service maze and was told "basically it was [his] fault that this happened," that nothing could be done because he didn't fill out a claim within 24 hours, and that the company would not respond further. The clip became a social media sensation and according to Carroll's website reached more than 150 million people and was the number one most-watched YouTube music video in the world in July 2009. Carroll also performed the song in Washington, DC, at a forum on passenger rights issues. The lesson, he says: social media means that "no customer is statistically insignificant" and that it's no longer acceptable for companies to get it right most of the time for most customers.

Crusading for Flyers' Rights: After sitting on the tarmac for nearly nine hours in 2006 without food, water, or information, Kate Hanni launched the website FlyersRights.org and started the Coalition for an Airline Passenger's Bill of Rights. *USA Today* has cited Hanni as "among the loudest voices calling for the government to hold airlines accountable for long delays that left fliers stuck onboard planes during long ground delays" and notes that the government instituted such a rule in late 2009 and airlines now face fines if passengers are stuck on board delayed flights for more than three hours without being given the option to get off the aircraft.

Winning in Small Claims Court: Bill Baker took JetBlue to small claims court and won in 2009 after the airline left him stranded by canceling his return flight from Portland, Oregon, following multiple delays that forced passengers to spend the night at the gate. The airline gave Baker a choice: accept a $229 refund along with a $100 voucher or take the next available JetBlue flight *three days later*. JetBlue refused to book Baker on a different plane, so, with all hotels Baker called booked solid, he paid $977 to fly back via Detroit on Northwest and Delta, started a blog, sued, and won. "I am just a guy who got tired of being abused by the airlines," said Baker. His advice: "If an airline screws you, do something about it. Take them to small claims court, start a blog, contact your congressman, picket the airline's headquarters, discover a new virus and name it after the airline. Whatever. Just do SOMETHING. The airlines will get away with whatever they can for as long as they can, as long as we let them."

IMPROVEMENTS SINCE THE GOLDEN AGE

While air travel certainly used to be a whole lot more fun, travelers have seen important improvements. If the travel and hospitality companies can just refocus on service, creating a customer experience that's better than ever is still a real possibility. Did you know:

- Airline ticket prices have fallen about 50 percent since 1978?

- Until the 1970s, you couldn't get seat assignments in advance?

- Live television, on-demand movies, a choice of music, Wi-Fi, and lie-flat seats all have been introduced since the Golden Age of jet travel?

- The planes of the old days were noisy and bumpy compared to today's jets?

- Smoking was permitted on some domestic flights prior to 1998?

5

We're No Better at Home

Hey baby, do you like fine cooking?
Cause you know what? I got a Swanson's
dinner in the freezer with your name on it.

—Jimmy Fallon

Health, marriage, and parenting are all suffering as we try to work 24-7 while raising above-average kids, giving back to the community, watching our cholesterol, firming our abs, connecting with our soul mate, and maintaining a sizzling sex life. Trying to be the best at everything is admirable, but it's also unrealistic.

What we're finding is that trying to do it all delivers mediocre results. Recognizing how out of reach our goals are, we give up midway. And instead we get indulged children, stressed parents, a workday that stretches into night, takeout food replacing home-cooked meals, and workout routines that consist primarily of taking the stairs up to bed. Where did we go wrong?

THE STRUGGLE TO BE GOOD PARENTS

Being a parent today is so different from 100 years ago or even 20 years ago. While our role hasn't changed, our approach to raising our kids has, and that hasn't been good for anyone.

Where our parents and grandparents emphasized obedience and service more than anything (remember the need to be "seen and not heard"?), today's parents are more concerned with over-providing freedom of expression and affection to their children. Researchers at Ohio State University who studied the impact that a mother's child-rearing style had on her children's parenting style found that today's mom is more likely to show affection regularly, express frequent praise, and read to her children three times as much as her mom did. "Freedom" seems to be the buzzword for today's parents, which was confirmed by another researcher who studied articles in *Parents* magazine through the ages. Markella Rutherford of Wellesley College reports that children today have more freedom to share opinions with parents but less freedom in the outside world, where rising safety concerns have curtailed a lot of unsupervised activities.

That said, ask any adults with children what their primary goal in life is and many will tell you it's "to be a good parent." That was certainly my goal as I raised a child from age three on my own. Perhaps modeling my own parents' style, I saw my role as protector, teacher, and disciplinarian, while other parents focused on being friends and allies with their children. Rather than setting rules and limits, they reveled in being unstructured and offering as much freedom as possible. This permissive parenting style may be more comfortable for some parents, but it sure has been bad for kids. Words such as "entitled" and "indulged" are thrown around a lot today, and even new words such as "affluenza" have emerged. (You're probably familiar with affluenza because it was famously used as a defense claim to explain why a drunk teen killed four people. Fingers are pointing at the parents for giving him too much freedom and too little guidance.)

Research has shown that indulged children are less self-disciplined and less responsible than children from families with clear guidelines and expectations for behavior. Without limits, kids rebel. Surprisingly, that rebellious behavior is often out of fear, as children and teens test to see when and whether mom and dad will respond to their bad behavior. Using surveys dating back to the 1930s, Jean Twenge, an associate professor of psychology at San Diego State University and author of *Generation Me*, has documented that today's children may be freer but they are also more anxious and depressed. Growing up in households where they have a say in nearly every decision becomes stressful for them, she found. The solution is to set boundaries, communicate rules, and be consistent in how rules are enforced.

Replacing discipline with complete freedom is dangerous, even criminal. Children who are not taught right from wrong, good behavior from bad, or how to make smart choices in everyday life struggle later. In actuality, kids who develop self-discipline are more likely to lead happier lives, thanks to a learned ability to manage conflict and emotional distress, according to a study published in the *Journal of Personality* in 2013.

In the extreme, you find examples such as Adam Lanza, who at age 20 opened fire on the Sandy Hook Elementary School, killing 26 people in 2012. With 20/20 hindsight, we can all wonder what Nancy Lanza, his mother, was thinking when she introduced her two young sons, Ryan and Adam, to guns and target shooting early in life. She and Adam, a troubled young boy, "bonded" over guns, she told friends. She also indulged his fascination with violent video games, which he spent most of his days playing. Without boundaries and parental guidance, children can get into a lot of trouble and hurt others in the process. Adam Lanza is a very sad case in point. I clearly remember the conflict when my son would want to play violent video games at a friend's house and I was completely opposed to it. Makes for being very unpopular.

Just as parenting today is a completely different experience from the one our parents had, childhood today is very different, too. In an effort to provide our children with every educational, athletic, musical, arts, and science-related opportunity known to humankind, we parents are working harder than ever. Single-income families are becoming rarer as both parents strive to earn enough to give their kids everything. While some financial stress may be reduced with both parents working, new challenges have emerged, such as finding time for family—or anything else, really.

A 2013 Pew Research Center survey found that 53 percent of all working parents with children under 18 say balancing the responsibilities of work with the responsibilities of their family is increasingly difficult. Even fewer are happy, the study found. Parents who say they do not spend enough time with their children, presumably because of work, are less happy than those who say they spend the right amount of time with their children . . . whatever "right" means.

Because of this demanding work schedule, children spend more time on their own than ever before. But they aren't completely alone; they have access to social media to keep them company. "Media becomes a surrogate parent. Perhaps Facebook is the new (bad) breast. The proliferation of technologies like social networking, cell phones, and video games have altered how children relate to significant others," says Molly Castelloe, PhD, in a 2011 *Psychology Today* article. Children are now relying on technology as their primary source of interaction and entertainment. Based on surveys of children ages 12 to 15, researchers at the U.S. Centers for Disease Control and Prevention found that nearly three-quarters spent at least two hours a day watching TV and using a computer. That's a lot of time alone, without personal interactions.

But what's a parent to do? In twenty-first-century America, 95 percent of dads and 90 percent of moms report having a work-family conflict, meaning they have difficulty managing both roles, reported Janet Gornick and Marcia Meyers in their book, *Families That Work: Policies for Reconciling Parenthood and Employment*. PepsiCo CEO Indra Nooyi has said that she finds it difficult to manage both her personal and professional demands. When parents feel squeezed by work and family commitments, the result is dissatisfaction on both fronts— and stress.

That doesn't necessarily mean that work is the primary cause of that stress, however. In fact, it's the opposite: work can be a respite from the demands of family life. A bigger stressor, or worry, is not measuring up at home. Researchers at Penn State found that "people have significantly lower levels of stress at work than at home," according to a research brief prepared by Sarah Damaske for the Council on Contemporary Families. Using the stress hormone cortisol as the indicator, researchers discovered that men and women were more stressed at home than at work and that women derived more stress-lowering benefit from work than men. This isn't a shocker, though, is it? We already knew that women handle most of the home-related responsibilities. On an average day in 2013, more women than men spent time doing household activities such as housework (83 percent of women versus 65 percent of men) and, when they did, women also spent more time on their household activities than men (2.6 hours for women versus 2.1 hours for men), according to the Bureau of Labor Statistics.

One of my major concerns with being a good mom (OK, it was everything!) included ensuring that my son was a good boy and that his behavior reflected that. So I impressed upon him the need to say please and thank-you when speaking, to be helpful, and to take the time to express appreciation by way of a thank-you note when it was warranted. Although these basic lessons should not have attracted any attention, they did. After playdates with other children, I would get compliments from friends about how polite and kind my son was. Not only had he been on his best behavior but also it was his typical behavior—yet it stood out. I felt proud and sad at the same time. Many parents have not taken the time to teach their children about proper behavior. They haven't given their kids the chance to be their best.

I think that's where we need to start in this attempt to break away from mediocrity and strive for excellence. Let's start with the little things, such as manners. Let's get back to the fundamentals of good behavior as parents.

TAKING CARE OF OUR HEALTH

We all know our healthcare system has problems. One sign is the average wait time to be seen by a doctor, even when you have an appointment. Recently, I arrived for a 9 a.m. doctor's appointment at 8:50 and didn't get put on the exam room table until 9:45. Then I waited some more. That's crazy. If I left my clients waiting for me for that amount of time on a scheduled meeting or call, I can promise they wouldn't be my clients for long. What's even worse is that the *lowest* average wait time nationwide in 2013 was 16 minutes, up from 15 minutes in 2011, according to *American Medical News*; this is expected to get worse and doesn't even include wait time in the exam room. Even when I'm a patient, my time should be considered valuable.

But what options do we have? Sure, we can get up and leave, just as we might do at a restaurant after waiting 55 minutes to place an order, but the problem is there are far too few doctors available to see us any more quickly. We just end up going to the end of the line at another doctor's office.

Even getting an appointment takes an average of 18 days, reports consulting firm Merritt Hawkins, but it can be as bad as 45.5 days if you live in Boston. Given Boston's high physician-per-capita figure, this can only be a sign of things to come. If it takes Bostonians 45 days to get an appointment with a physician, imagine the wait in more remote locations. (I'm kind of scared for residents of, say, Alaska.)

Many doctors today are in such demand that they triple or even quadruple book themselves in order to fit more patients into their day.

The result is that *we* wait. We endure the poor service. Of course, if we're more than a few minutes late to an appointment, we have to reschedule. Accepting bad service from our healthcare providers has become increasingly commonplace.

After all, they are in the power position. We need them, and there are fewer of them to go around. A 2013 CNBC report found that the United States is short about 16,000 primary care doctors. That means about 55 million people are without a doctor or are having difficulty finding one simply because there aren't enough to go around. The American Association of Medical Colleges predicted in 2010 that by 2020, that physician shortage would balloon to 90,000. Exacerbating the situation is that of doctors currently in practice, nearly half of the 830,000 are over age 50 and scaling back the number of patients they are seeing, according to a 2012 Physicians Foundation Survey. I don't blame them; I might want to be working less as I approach retirement, too.

Demand for doctor services is also growing, with an estimated eight million more people retiring every day. The world is getting older and in need of more medical care than ever before. And with the Affordable Care Act adding 30 million more patients to the pool, demands on doctors' time will only get worse.

So what can we do to avoid having to make more trips to the doctor? Take control of our own health. Making better choices about what we're eating, getting more exercise, and reducing risky behaviors such as smoking are all good places to start. We need to take personal responsibility for preserving our own health. As of today, we're not doing a very good job.

We're not alone, if that makes you feel any better. A survey conducted by the Institute for Health Metrics and Evaluation (IHME) at the University of Washington reported that the world as a whole is getting heavier. Nearly 30 percent of the global population is overweight or obese now, as a result of obesity rates that have been, uh, expanding since 1980. In the United States, 160 million Americans are either obese or overweight, and by 2030, says a

2012 study published in the *Journal of Preventive Medicine*, 42 percent of the country will be obese.

Given this statistic, it's not surprising that too few adults are taking steps to curb the growth of their waistline. The Centers for Disease Control and Prevention reported in 2012 that only 20.3 percent of adults 18 years and older met the organization's physical activity guidelines for both aerobic physical and muscle-strengthening activity.

Not only is obesity causing health conditions such as heart disease and diabetes but also it's creating issues with respect to access to health care. A 2013 NBC story reported on the rising number of patients being denied air ambulance service as a result of their weight and size. An estimated 1 percent of the 500,000 patients requiring medical air flights each year are denied transport because of their inability to fit through the plane's doors or because they exceed the helicopter's weight and size limits.

Fortunately, a lot of employers are making it easier for employees to try to live healthier lives. More than 85 percent of U.S. companies with 1,000 employees or more offer some kind of workplace wellness program, reports a recent RAND Corporation study. Many programs are multifaceted, offering wellness screening activities to identify health risks as well as "interventions" to prevent diseases and chronic health conditions. Of the organizations offering wellness programs, nearly 80 percent offer nutrition and weight loss activities, such as on-site Weight Watchers meetings and *Biggest Loser*–type weight loss competitions, while 77 percent offer some type of smoking cessation program, including educational programs or telephone counseling.

Part of the reason for offering such wellness programs is selfish—healthier employees cost the company less in healthcare costs, are more productive, and take fewer sick days—but some employers also care about their employees as people. Several of my company's employees, for example, sit on balance balls at their desks to improve their posture and get a core workout even while seated. Also, it's kind of fun to sit on a big bouncy ball. Then they take walks at lunch to break up the day and get their heart pumping. Other companies have similar initiatives. Perhaps you'd like to work at L.L. Bean, where employees can take Zumba and yoga classes. Intuit has a "Workout on Wheels" cart, which offers employees 15-minute mini-workouts combining strengthening, stretching, and relaxation. Our office doesn't have a workout cart, but I have a standing desk myself to try to eliminate being in a seated position for too long, and I've offered this arrangement to anyone in the company who wants it.

Companies are stepping up to try to encourage healthier lifestyles, but in the end, it's up to us, the individual. Despite being given access to fitness facilities, fun workout sessions, and incentives, employees don't take advantage of these amenities primarily because of lack of time, says a *Modern Healthcare* article. Employers create part of the problem, and some are starting to realize this. As a result of a banking intern dying from overwork, Bank of America Merrill Lynch in early 2014 issued a mandate that junior banking employees needed to take at least four days a month to rest. While at other companies, where employees regularly take eight weekend days off a month, this might sound like punishment to those in the banking industry: insisting that employees take a break is a new way of thinking. It's also pretty scary, if you think about it. How are they functioning if they never take days off? And what's the big appeal of the banking industry (other than piles of money) if you're denied sleep? These work restrictions are certainly a step in the right direction.

The fact of the matter is we're getting sicker because of our own choices. Did you know that the average American consumes 130 pounds of sugar each year, according to the documentary *Fed Up*? We're poisoning ourselves by eating as much processed food and drinking as many sodas as we do. As I write this book, I've been sugar-free for almost a year—not easy!

New York's former Mayor Michael Bloomberg tried to help by instituting a citywide ban on sodas larger than 16 ounces, but instead of cheering him for trying to impose some commonsense limits, residents were up in arms.

"Why does the government have the power to tell us how much carbonated soda we're allowed to drink?" people seemed to ask. My response is that until we get better at regulating our own sugar addiction, someone needs to be the voice of reason. Ultimately, the state overturned it. Current NYC Mayor Bill de Blasio recently announced that he would reintroduce the ban, if for no other reason than to encourage parents to have conversations with their children about healthy eating and drinking habits. To get healthy, we need to make changes, no matter how delicious those cronuts are. We need to think more carefully about what we put in our bodies on a regular basis. Ice cream once in a while won't kill you, but a daily Big Gulp just might.

First Lady Michelle Obama is doing her best to improve the quality of food served during school lunch periods, but she may have gone a bit too far in her guidelines. Children are eating more fruits and vegetables in schools, found a Harvard School of Public Health study, but participation in the National School Lunch Program is down 3.7 percent during the 2012–2013 school year, according to the Government Accountability Office, because of the heavy vegetable emphasis. Children simply aren't buying as many lunches thanks to the new guidelines, and schools are increasingly opting out as a result. This may have been a case of too much change too fast and children are voting with their lunch money. Schools can't afford the higher costs for food their students can't afford or won't eat, yet changing our diet needs to happen—and quickly. We need to find some middle ground.

What we eat may also be affecting the illnesses that we Americans are being diagnosed with and at younger ages. Asthma cases are up, food allergies are through the roof, and behavioral conditions continue to rise. Is it due to our diet? It's certainly possible. Reported cases of ADHD have increased 42 percent since 2003, according to a study published in the *American Academy of Child and Adolescent Psychiatry*. Eleven percent of children between the ages of four and 17 have been diagnosed with ADHD, and 6 percent are being medicated for it. Those are big numbers. Viewed as a biological disorder in the United States, ADHD is treated with medicine here. However, in France, where the incidence of ADHD is just 0.5 percent, the treatment provided is psychotherapy and family counseling, to get at the root cause of the behavior.

Experts concur that what we eat determines the likelihood of developing heart disease, diabetes, and cancers. *The China Study*, by Dr. T. Colin Campbell, professor emeritus at Cornell University, is a groundbreaking book published in 2005 that reports that a diet rich in animal proteins—meat and dairy—was more likely to result in chronic and terminal illnesses than a plant-based diet more common in Eastern countries such as China.

We can't overhaul our health overnight, but we can surely make small strides in important areas such as diet and exercise, the two underpinnings of good health.

DEEPENING OUR PERSONAL CONNECTIONS

We're also setting ourselves up for failure in our personal lives by creating expectations that no human could ever live up to.

It's happening primarily within marriages, as Chin Ming Hui, Kathleen Carswell, Grace Larson, and Eli Finkel report in a recent *New York Times* article titled "The All-or-Nothing Marriage." "Americans today have elevated their expectations of marriage," the researchers state. Those individuals who are willing to invest time and energy in a partnership can achieve much higher than average satisfaction in their relationship, and those who won't invest won't get—which helps explain why a full 45 percent of all marriages currently end in divorce. In many cases, we're setting our partners and ourselves up for failure by expecting the relationship to be beyond perfect. The reality is that few are but that with work they can be great—maybe not perfect but satisfying and emotionally fulfilling.

Marriages aren't the only relationships that are weaker today. Unfortunately, the quality and depth of friendships seem to be weakening, too. We can place part of the blame on technology, of course, but impossibly

69

high expectations are also a factor. Expecting, or demanding, too much from our friends and loved ones can damage those ties as well.

Oddly enough, we think we're actually more socially connected than ever. Social media sites such as Facebook, Twitter, LinkedIn, Instagram, and Snapchat provide a false sense of engagement with others. Sending e-mails and texts isn't really the same as having a face-to-face conversation, no matter how many times we may try to tell ourselves that. Sitting across from someone at a table and having coffee while reminiscing about that time you got a hole in one or the funniest thing your kid said last week—those are real conversations.

Some people use social media like it's their job. Seventy percent of adults who are online spend an average of 23 hours per week reading e-mail, texting, and checking on social media—as much as a part-time job, points out the lifestyle blog Fix.com. Being, and staying, connected to the Internet has become an addiction for the vast majority of smartphone owners.

But if being connected to our friends via social media were a good thing, we'd probably feel a whole lot better about it than we do. A study from the University of Salford in the United Kingdom found that 50 percent of people who use Facebook and Twitter feel worse about themselves after reading all the impressive status updates their friends are posting: "Just met the Queen of England—she wants to do lunch!" or "Thinking of ditching my penthouse on Park Avenue for a Miami mansion." It's completely understandable why our self-esteem takes a hit after monitoring what everyone else is saying about his or her fabulous life. Some of us are getting a little fed up with all this oversharing, too. According to research by Pew in 2014, 36 percent of Facebook users really hate it when you share too much. It's OK to talk about how proud you are of your daughter who was just accepted to Yale, but do you have to tell everyone she was valedictorian of her class, was named a member of the 2018 Alpine ski team, and last week cured a form of cancer? It's a bit much. We can take only so much inadequacy.

Sometimes it's not the what but the when that irritates us. Princeton Survey Research Associates found that 25 percent of cell phone owners in serious relationships reported that the device got in the way of connecting with their partner when they were alone and that it was distracting. We're so concerned about missing out on an online conversation that 80 percent of us grab our smartphone to check in within 15 minutes of waking up; some of us don't even bother to get out of bed first. That's dedication. According to the Mobile Mindset Study of 2012, 60 percent of those surveyed admitted they don't go an hour without checking their phone; 40 percent even check their phone while on the toilet. (I sure hope they don't flush while on a call.)

Talking on a cell phone also makes us oblivious to what's going on around us. "The use of cell phones affects helping behavior," found a group of *Discover* magazine researchers who tested how willing people would be to help someone in need. Only 9 percent of people who were talking on their cell phone offered help, versus 72 percent of those who were not. The conclusion? We can be jerks when we're on our phones.

The reality is that by communicating less face-to-face, our relationships overall are suffering. They have changed as a result of technology. The whole center of our relationships has shifted from being physically present to being remotely present. Because of this, the next generation has a distorted sense of what a real relationship is—who has 1,000 friends, as we see on Facebook? They think an online-only connection is just as deep as an in-person bond.

A viral video titled "Look Up" that debuted in 2014 addresses this situation head-on, urging viewers to "live life the real way"—meaning through face-to-face conversations and in-person get-togethers, not obsessively connected to the Internet. With more than 46 million views to date, this video's message has touched a nerve.

While technology is coming between many relationships, it's also rekindling others, but not always in a good way. As of 2010, 20 percent of all divorces involve Facebook, according to a survey by the American Academy of Matrimonial Lawyers. Social media is also increasingly being called into evidence in such cases. Technology generally has made it much easier to identify bad behavior. Even when you're not misbehaving, excessive use can predict future troubles, a University of Missouri PhD student found. He linked the use of Twitter to heightened conflict, cheating, and divorce.

But bad behavior isn't limited to romantic relationships. Threats, nasty comments, and inappropriate photos shared online have led to death threats, lawsuits, and job loss, to name only a handful of cases. Because of the rising incidence of slander, libel, defamation, or invasion of privacy claims, personal injury endorsement insurance coverage is now an option, because when defendants lose in such cases, they tend to lose big. By 2012, 36 verdicts related to things people said and did online cost insurers nearly $87 million.

Unfortunately, bad behavior online is also hard to cover up. More companies are now paying as much as $15,000 to Kroll Background Screening for an in-depth social media history on key executive job candidates—better safe than sorry. And 31 percent of college admissions officers look at applicants' social media accounts as part of the decision-making process, found Kaplan Test Prep. That's a scary thought for some high-school students and their parents.

Taking a step back, whether we're talking about parenting styles, career goals, relationships, or golf swings, is smart. Pro golfer Rory McIlroy recognized a need to go back to the fundamentals of his game after signing a new sponsorship deal with Nike. Leaving behind former sponsor Titleist for Nike meant switching from the Titleist clubs he had been playing and winning with to a set of Nikes. The transition was anything but smooth. Soon after making the switch, he withdrew from the 2013 Honda Classic, where he was playing poorly.

To his credit, McIlroy recognized the need for change. The way he was swinging his new clubs, which was the way he swung his old clubs, was no longer effective. He needed to relearn how to hit the ball. At the time, his caddy expected that it might take a few months: a few months of training in order to reap the benefits for years to come. Sounds like a good choice. Clearly, it's paying off; in 2014 he won the British Open and the Bridgestone Invitational and became the world's top-ranked player and PGA champion.

When things aren't working, getting back to basics makes sense: recalibrating and making corrections, returning to fundamentals such as self-discipline, respect, and polite behavior, all of which need to be revisited and retaught if we want our children to truly be their best and have better health and more satisfying relationships.

So how can you be a better, healthier parent, friend, and partner? Here are some suggestions for doing more of what makes you happier and limiting behavior that can get you in trouble, online and off.

10 WAYS TO BE YOUR BEST

1. *Think before You Post*: Sure, that photo of you on a yacht is great, but is it really the message you want to send your shareholders after watching your company's stock price tank? Or that selfie you took for fun last week with the exotic dancer—do you really want everyone to know what you've been up to on your own time? And just because Kim Kardashian made it big following the release of her sex tape does not mean you'll be as lucky—better keep yours private. Your children also need to understand that absolutely everything they share online will be visible to everyone, forever. So be careful about what you share, and educate your children about what they make public, to protect your reputation and those you care about.

2. *Wait to Upload*: When in doubt, take the photo but don't share it on Instagram or Facebook just yet. If you're mad or drunk or tired, save it until you have a clearer head. Then consider the potential impression you'll be sending to those who have access to it. Drunken photos won't help your child custody case, if you know what I mean. We need to get better at filtering ourselves and our public behavior.

3. *Invest Time in Your Relationships*: To develop and maintain strong, healthy relationships that are good for you and for others, you need to put in the time—and not just on Facebook or by phone. You need to see each other and talk face-to-face so you can pick up on body language and facial expressions and get a true sense of how people you care about are doing. Make time for them.

4. *Move*: Research is increasingly showing how damaging sitting at a desk all day can be. So take every opportunity to get up and move around. You don't have to go for a daily run, though it would certainly be healthy, but stretch your legs and walk around every chance you get.

5. *Go Organic*: Just as sitting has been found to be bad for our hearts and our backsides, research shows that eating pesticide-laden food is also bad for our health. Buying and consuming organic produce, meat, and dairy helps reduce the chemicals we ingest.

6. *Put Your Phone Down*: Years ago a Chicago hotel offered to put personal communications devices under lock and key for guests who wanted a break. They may have been on to something. We all check our phones constantly, but in addition to raising our stress levels unnecessarily, it's getting in the way of conversations and relationships we could be having. So let's all put our phones away unless we're expecting a call. Focus on the person in front of you who is eager to connect with you. Give that person your attention, not your smartphone; it won't ever make you feel as good as your friends will.

7. *Get Back to Fundamentals*: When things don't seem to be working as well as they should, take a breather. Think back to a better time and try to remember what was different. While we are all moving at the speed of sound, a back-to-basics approach can be very satisfying.

8. *Become Goal Oriented Personally—and Write It Down!* We can accomplish just so many personal things in a day, a week, a month, or a year. Many of us profess our business goals but don't do the same for our personal lives. Focus on things you want to accomplish for you, your children, and your relationships. You may not get to everything, but at least you have a road map that will help you get closer to what's really important to you. This could be a weekly date with your spouse, a movie night with your children, or how many days at the gym you find necessary to get to your health goals.

9. *Give Yourself the Luxury of a Mentor or Coach*: People with a wealth of experience and expertise can share information and lend guidance as you move ahead.

10. *No One Is Perfect*: Remember there is no such thing as perfection. Our socks may not match, and we may forget things because we are under so much pressure to deliver in every aspect of our lives. After all, we are only human! One of my colleagues remembers a day when he wore two different-colored shoes to the office. Give yourself permission to make mistakes, but let's try not to repeat them too often.

6

The Death of Corporate Responsibility

**There's no one who wants this over more than I do.
I'd like my life back.**

—BP then-CEO Tony Hayward on the 2010 disaster that killed
11 people and caused the largest oil spill in U.S. history

nspired by the "my bad" mind-set, the corporate world has jumped into the Mediocre Revolution with both feet, thus generating results ranging from the ridiculous, such as Lululemon's former CEO Chip Wilson suggesting that the problem with his company's subpar yoga pants wasn't that they were defective but that fat women were wearing them, to the deadly, as with the General Motors (GM) decade-plus recall delay. So what started companies down the slippery slope from rudeness to negligence and fatalities?

It started with lies—lies that companies told themselves and then told their customers: from "This is a revolutionary idea that will turn our company's fortunes around" to "This is totally legal" to "Just don't tell anyone about the problem." Few companies start out as fraudulent, but as the lies pile up, behavior shifts to cover up the lies, and that's when consumers get hurt.

Fewer and fewer companies seem to care about their customers; they've lost touch, viewing patrons and customers not as important individuals in their own right but more as sources of profit. The quality of customer service provided in all industries has nosedived as companies have all but stopped trying to please the people who pay them money for goods and services. They've stooped to lying—to themselves and others—to justify their profit focus.

THE LIES WE'RE TOLD

The biggest lies being told in recent memory have to do with money (no surprise, right?) and using tricky accounting to cover up bad news and highlight good news that may or may not actually exist. Accounting scandals became rampant in the 1990s and early 2000s as companies either plotted to deceive or simply made use of legitimate accounting practices but in an unethical way. Between 1967 and 1990, the United States had a grand total of three accounting scandals. In the next 13 years, between 1991 and 2004, there were 36 such scandals, which hurt businesses and consumers to the tune of billions, and perhaps even trillions, of dollars. That doesn't even include the more recent Bernie Madoff scandal.

Just look at Enron, which *Fortune* magazine named "America's Most Innovative Company" six years in a row and which ultimately went bankrupt in 2001. That "innovative company" cost many investors their life savings. What happened at Enron involved basically taking advantage of tax accounting loopholes to hide liabilities. If you throw all your bills into a drawer and lock it, your checking account may look flush with cash, but the reality is that you still have to pay those bills, and they will eventually come due. That's what happened at Enron: CEO Kenneth Lay and COO Jeffrey Skilling came up with some crafty accounting practices through the use of limited liability special purpose entities and made it possible for management to hide those bills away, far from the eyes of investors and credit rating agencies. So the value of the company and stock continued to climb as its hidden debt was growing even faster. Once the liabilities were discovered in 2001, however, the company was all but worthless, and Skilling, who had been promoted to CEO, was headed for a 14-year prison sentence.

Bernie Ebbers, former CEO of WorldCom, famously claimed not to know that his subordinates were cooking the books—a.k.a. "improperly recording sales expenditures"—at the telecom giant. The fact that the company made 70 acquisitions in five years should have been a clue that the business was growing through questionable means. And when WorldCom declared bankruptcy in 2002, after being outed by an internal auditor for its deceptive practices, not only did shareholders and employees lose but also suppliers and competitors lost, because they had been trying to keep pace with a company that was not playing fair—and winning. Total cost? Around $11 billion. Ebbers, too, is now in prison for the foreseeable future. Ultimately, the lies employees told themselves and the outside world hurt everyone.

Investors in Bernie Madoff's hedge fund lost an estimated $65 billion, thanks to an enormous Ponzi scheme he created perhaps as far back as 1972 and continued to run until 2008. Thanks to our own collective belief that reading financial statements is nearly impossible for the average investor, few of his investors ever did read them. Nor did they check dates on which trades were supposedly made, some of which were reported for days the market was closed, or the trading values, which sometimes were far off what the stock was selling for. In short, Madoff lied for years, expected to have been caught long ago, and, frankly, was surprised that no one checked his bold-faced lies. He, too, is in jail, but only around half the money his investors lost has been recovered. Having dear friends who are personally affected by this every day makes it that much more devastating.

Homeowners got hurt during the mortgage crisis of 2008, which kicked off a global recession deeper than almost any since the Great Depression. They got hurt because the financial industry assumed that housing values would always appreciate. Despite economic facts, companies lied to themselves, reassuring everyone within earshot that mortgages were among the safest investments around. Standards for approving mortgages declined and guidelines loosened because no one worried that the value of properties being financed would ever significantly decline; little things such as proof of income and property assessments were fudged to get consumers the homes they would love to have but that were clearly beyond their means. And then after issuing mortgages to subprime borrowers and discovering that they couldn't necessarily afford the massive mortgages they had been given, the financial industry collapsed. New terms entered our lexicon, such as "underwater" and "upside down," and foreclosures became an everyday occurrence.

Perhaps what makes such behavior even more maddening is that so few of these corporate liars take responsibility or seem to feel that they're accountable in any way. They play the blame game or claim not to have known about the illegal acts. Or, in the case of Madoff, they simply have no remorse—he doesn't even pretend to feel sorry about what he did. We have hardly even heard a "my bad" out of him. That may be the scariest thing of all.

Sadly, unethical behavior within corporations appears to be on the rise. One of the lead whistleblowers in WorldCom's $3.8-billion accounting scandal, Cynthia Cooper, advised students at the McCombs School of Business at the University of Texas at Austin: "It's important to prepare yourselves now for the ethical dilemmas you'll face in the workplace. Because it's not if—it's when." I have heard her speak in person, and, wow, it's really scary to understand what takes place in these corporate environments gone askew.

Ultimately, these lies have damaged the trust customers place in others: from doctors to financial advisors, from to car salespeople to dry cleaners, from accountants to waiters. Does anyone have your best interests at heart? Mistakes happen, but organizations that take our money and call us their customers must have better compliance and better governance.

MONEY ABOVE ALL ELSE

Let me just say up front that I have absolutely no problem with companies making a profit. Money is what determines whether our economy is healthy, and it pays for things we need and want. But when maximizing profits becomes more important than everything else, everyone's health and safety are jeopardized—mine and yours. This is true whether we're talking about physical health, financial health, or emotional health or about Americans, Russians, or Aussies. Cutting corners or looking the other way at improper behavior hurts us all.

The crises we keep hearing about in the financial services industry are certainly a prime example. Ponzi schemes, as with Mr. Madoff, while rare, are becoming more common, as advisors take advantage of their expert status to dupe their clients. Just look at some of the rules now in place that give an advantage to those advisors who are supposed to have our backs. Did you know that when your advisor recommends a particular stock, it may be because the parent organization has decided to sell some off and is looking for a willing buyer? It's hard to know who is telling the truth and who isn't. Just look at food safety.

We have seen an increasing number of issues with our food supply. The Centers for Disease Control and Prevention (CDC) estimates that every year 48 million Americans, or one in six people in the United States, get sick from foodborne illnesses, 128,000 are hospitalized, and 3,000 die. Now, certainly, our ability to test for bacteria has improved dramatically in the past few decades, so it would make sense that we would see an increase simply because of our testing capabilities, and some level of bacteria is normal. However, some of what is being found should never have been in the food supply to begin with.

In a scandal that came to light in 2009, three hundred and ninety-nine people in 42 states were sickened by salmonella discovered in five-pound vats of peanut butter distributed through King Nut to food service operations. The peanut butter was recalled, though thankfully none had been sold directly to consumers. What caused the outbreak? I don't think we ever heard.

We do know what happened when salmonella again appeared, this time in eggs. August 2010 saw the largest recorded outbreak since the CDC began testing for it in the early 1970s: more than 550 million eggs had to be recalled due to *Salmonella enteritidis*. The owners of Quality Eggs were later indicted and fined for various misdeeds, the most egregious of which was labeling eggs as fresher than they actually were. They were able to do that, however, because of *bribes* they paid to a public official to ignore the poor quality. This outbreak could have been easily prevented.

A year later, nearly two million pounds of ground beef possibly tainted with a strain of *E. coli* was voluntarily recalled after 11 people became ill after eating it. The source was never identified, but to avoid sickening others, the distributor pulled the meat off grocers' shelves. I respect the company, Wolverine Packing Co., for taking this costly step in the name of health and safety: it didn't hesitate to question whether the choice was worth the price, and it didn't make excuses for how the beef had become tainted; it simply and quickly recalled the product.

This move comes in stark contrast to European meat distributors who had been sneaking (presumably less expensive) horsemeat into their ground beef packages. Theirs was clearly a business decision to supplement the ground beef with horsemeat rather than unlucky exposure to rare bacteria. I mean, how else could the horsemeat have gotten into the ground beef? Did thousands of horses slip and fall into the grinder by accident? Not likely.

And as a result of their dishonesty, a long list of companies had to recall products and issue apologies to their customers who had (unbeknownst to them) eaten the hybrid meat.

The food industry isn't the only sector to be experiencing a sharp drop in customer focus or quality of service, unfortunately. We're seeing an uptick in mistakes made in health care, too, with doctors making routine errors when caring for patients.

In fact, 1,500 patients are the victims of careless physician errors each year, reports the *New England Journal of Medicine*. A 2008 study conducted by the *Annals of Surgery* reported that medical instruments or materials are left behind in one out of 7,000 surgeries. So of the 51.4 million surgeries conducted in 2010, according to CDC statistics, that means that in 7,343 of them, stuff was left behind. Some items I can almost understand, such as cotton balls or gauze, but a *13-inch surgical retractor*? Yes, that was left behind after a man had abdominal surgery. (Personally, I would have thought that would be pretty hard to miss.) Or what about the case of a woman who had arthroscopic surgery who continued to have problems because a needle had been left behind? Another woman who experienced ongoing issues after a hysterectomy discovered that the cause was a surgical glove that was left behind in her uterus. Not only are these mistakes stupid but also they cause continued pain and suffering for the patients who turn to their doctors for relief from their pain. Leaving items behind isn't the only type of healthcare mistake being made, however. Doctors are also operating on the wrong body parts and the wrong patient 20 times a week, on average, reported *Surgery* in 2012. I heard a story recently about a woman who had been diagnosed with two lumps in her breast, one malignant and one benign. The surgeons went in and took out . . . yes, you guessed it, the benign lump. Needless to express, this case caused extraordinary pain and suffering.

Saturday Night Live alum Dana Carvey went in to the hospital for a double bypass operation and discovered later that the surgeon had bypassed the wrong artery. The doctor claimed the error was an honest mistake that could have happened to anyone—essentially the equivalent of saying "oops." That "oops" resulted in a $7.5-million lawsuit.

Another poor man in Rhode Island turned to a doctor for help in stemming bleeding on his brain. The doctor performed a CAT scan, confirmed the bleeding was on the left side of the brain, and proceeded moments later to drill into the right side of the man's skull. Oops again. The patient recovered fully, thank goodness. Willie King of Tampa, Florida, was not so lucky. King went to the hospital to have his leg amputated, and doctors amputated the wrong one.

While these are extreme examples, even more routine errors occur on a regular basis with respect to medications. A doctor intended to administer to a nine-year-old child medication to treat an infection following an appendectomy and instead gave a dose of intravenous antifungal medication meant for a full-grown adult. The patient went into cardiac arrest and had to be resuscitated. She recovered and sued the hospital for nearly $4 million. Another incident of poor care occurred at a fertility treatment center, where, instead of being impregnated with her husband's DNA, a woman was given the sperm of a stranger of a different ethnicity. The mistake wasn't discovered until the child was born, of course. Oops.

I'm not saying that mistakes don't happen—they do—but I am saying that mistakes are happening more frequently these days and no one seems too concerned. Rarely do we even hear any expression of remorse from people who have made mistakes. Instead, we hear lawyers offering excuses and explanations.

THE PRICE OF HIDING A PROBLEM

Part of the problem may be that companies equate admitting mistakes with expensive lawsuits. Sure, whistleblowers may be exempt from prosecution if they report a bad act, but if you yourself get caught, is it better to admit an error or deny, deny, deny? The consensus seems to be that denial is the way to go.

For years, doctors in training were frequently required to attend classes taught by attorneys on what to do if they made a mistake in treating a patient. Apologizing is at the bottom of the list of things to do; in fact, in some cases, apologizing voids insurance coverage because it is tantamount to admitting guilt. To me, this seems like it could only make the situation worse. No accountability or responsibility required of physicians, or attorneys, or financial advisors means less time and attention paid to their patients or customers. If you're not expected to do your absolute best, with repercussions if you don't, what's the incentive to give it your all? There is none.

And yet the companies that are willing to immediately step up, admit there was a problem, take responsibility, and indicate what's being done about it are much better off. Their customers are better off, too. It's when companies try to deflect attention or responsibility, pointing to scapegoats to explain what went wrong, that we have a real problem. GM is a case in point.

In February 2013, GM recalled 2.6 million of its cars, mainly Chevrolet Cobalts and Saturn Ions, because of a defective ignition switch. Thirteen people have died as of this writing as a result of the engine randomly shutting off, leaving the driver not in control of the power steering or brakes. Recalls are not unusual or uncommon, but this one was because it took more than 10 years for GM to even admit there was a problem (the first claims of issues were made in 2003). What's even more distressing is that those deaths could have been prevented, and the problem corrected, with a 57-cent part plus labor costs. GM had apparently allowed below-standard ignition switches to be used in manufacturing, which created the problem, but a corrective part that cost less than a dollar could have been incorporated.

If the recall had occurred back in 2007, a few years after the problem had been discovered, it would have cost GM $100 million. GM decided that was too much money to spend at the time. The recall, repairs, and pending lawsuits will certainly cost multiples of that figure today, seven years later, not to mention the congressional inquiry currently occurring. Damage to GM's brand is certainly well above the $100-million mark.

So what could the company have done differently? Take accountability with the injured drivers' families, issue a recall, fix the problem, and reassure drivers that GM is ahead of this issue and doing everything in its power to keep its customers safe. Most recently, CEO Mary Barra has taken steps in the right direction.

What GM should have done was too expensive, however, so now it can pay into the billions because it decided to keep the problems a secret.

Unfortunately, this issue with the ignition switch is not the first incident of GM keeping defects a secret. The Chevy Malibu's gas tank placement made it more likely to explode in an accident, yet GM decided it was not in the company's best interests to make this public. Estimating that deaths from postcollision fuel tank fires would cost the company $2.40 per car (assuming the value of a person's life at $200,000), GM continued to sell the Chevy Malibu. What's even more infuriating is that GM designers had developed a solution to fix the problem that would have cost $8.59 per car, but since that number was more than the $2.40 to leave it as is, GM left the car design as is.

Automakers have a short-term mind-set. They compare the costs of doing nothing short-term with the costs of a recall and repair, which are almost always higher than doing nothing—hence the reason so many people are hurt and killed before pressure builds that forces manufacturers to make changes.

THE HIGH COST OF BAD CUSTOMER SERVICE

Companies with a short-term mind-set are the ones most likely to provide the worst customer service and, therefore, the most likely to go out of business sooner rather than later. They aren't aiming to provide their best products and services, only something customers won't complain about. Their standards are low, and it shows. In some cases, it costs customers their lives; in others, it simply costs the business a customer.

Companies that consider the lifetime value of customers typically work harder to hold onto them; attracting them probably costs a pretty penny, so smart companies do their best not to lose them once they have them. Just look at Wegmans Food Markets, whose ardent fans consistently rate it among the best grocery chains in the country; Southwest Airlines, known for its excellent service built on good humor; and Harley-Davidson, whose motorcycles remain the most coveted worldwide, in part because of its fabulous service. Striving to provide excellent customer service has always been my firm's approach, so I'm always surprised when companies I patronize seem to care so little about making sure I'm a satisfied customer.

Recently, my husband and I and another couple went out for dinner at a restaurant we've been to before. The meals are always good, so we felt confident we'd enjoy a nice night out together. While the company of the other couple was delightful, the service we received was not. It took an hour for our salads to be served and another whole hour to get our entrees.

It was after 11:00 by the time we finished our meals and had paid our check. We had been seated at 7:30. Only at the end of the evening did the owner come over to sheepishly offer us an after-dinner drink on the house for our wait. An after-dinner drink for making us wait more than two hours for our food? Too little, too late. If he had been concerned about satisfying his customers—us—he should have given us the meal for free, or at least taken some of the meals off the bill. Instead, he offered us a free drink at the bar long after we wanted to go home. To demonstrate how much he valued us as customers wouldn't have taken much—the cost of the meal to him was maybe $50 or so—and, in turn, we would have been so delighted with his apology and show of appreciation that we probably would have dined there even more often than we had in the past.

While the owner may have been paid in full for the meals he served us that night, they will be the last he ever serves us. We won't go back. He made the full $150 on the cost of the dinner, but he lost out on the thousands of dollars we would have spent in the coming years as frequent guests and word-of-mouth advocates. That's what I mean about a short-term mind-set. Taking a loss now to compensate for a poor customer experience is better than insisting on being paid in full and then losing that customer for good. That's not a good outcome for anyone.

REBUILDING TRUST

Accepting mediocrity as a business philosophy is costing some companies customers and sometimes costing customers their lives. This isn't OK. We need to raise our expectations of companies we patronize and communicate those expectations to them.

When companies let us down by providing poor service or selling us defective products, we need to hold them accountable. They need to make reparations and to demonstrate that they accept responsibility for their poor decisions and are willing to make amends. We need to demand apologies and admissions of guilt when appropriate. And we need to be willing to make those apologies and admissions ourselves.

It's the fundamental adage of treating others the way we would like to be treated. We wouldn't want to be lied to or treated as if we don't matter by the companies we give our money to, so we need to start modeling that behavior. By being our best, we can raise the bar for companies we do business with.

10 STEPS TO MAKING THE CUSTOMER NUMBER ONE AGAIN

1. *Know Your Customer:* Know who your typical customers are, as well as your "regulars." Nothing does more to solidify a relationship with your customers than making them feel special. Let them know that you've paid

attention and know their name and their preferences—such as how they like their meal cooked or their shirts pressed. In the case of my bank, I get a welcoming and resounding "Hello, Julie!" when I walk into the branch. All it takes is a little focused attention.

2. *Be Connected to Your Customers*: Being connected is twofold: (1) staying in touch and (2) really paying attention to them when they are in your presence. Take note of what's going on in their life, what you may be able to assist them with, or how you can make their life easier. Listen for those nuggets of information and the subsequent opportunity to assist them. Then stay in touch with an e-mail or a quick note dropped in the mail. Let them know you're thinking of them—that they matter. As a rule, I like to wish many of my clients happy birthday, and I have most of them on my calendar, because it matters and I care.

3. *Claim Excellence as a Motto*: Too many people have become comfortable with mediocrity. Doing what's minimally expected is commonplace nowadays. So set yourself apart by striving to do more than what's expected. Exceed expectations by delivering more than you promised. That could mean finishing the work you promised your client a week early or even a day early. It could mean consistently achieving 0 percent defects or errors in your products. Or maybe excellence in your business is providing an added bonus, such as an enlargement of your clients' favorite wedding photo that you took, at no charge. Excellence is unexpected today, so find a way to go above and beyond, to set yourself apart from the mediocre.

4. *Acknowledge Problems When They Occur and Not a Moment Later*: Our instinctive reaction to a problem is to distance ourselves or to claim no involvement. We're more worried about making sure everyone knows it was not our fault than we are about taking responsibility and focusing on what we can do for those affected. To give your best, you need to first acknowledge the problem. Even if you can't give specific details and you don't know what went wrong or why, at least admit that there is an issue and you're working on it. Don't wait until you have all the information. Instead, share what you have and reassure customers that you're aware of the problem and are already trying to address it. That creates more goodwill and trust than anything.

5. *Understand That Customer Loyalty Is Earned*: Attracting a new customer is a major accomplishment. Celebrate that whenever it occurs. It means your marketing program is working: it's enticing and persuading people to do business with you. But doing business with you once does not necessarily translate to repeat business. To ensure that customers come back again and again, you need to continue to provide excellent products and services. That consistency of quality is what helps build customer loyalty. Customer loyalty builds over time the more you exceed customer expectations, but recognize that one-time customers are not necessarily loyal customers. You have to earn their business each and every time they have a need for the products or services your company provides.

6. *Actions Speak Louder* than *Words*: Be someone who shows how important your customers are by doing what you say you will. It starts with integrity and being a person or company of your word. Don't make promises unless you plan to keep them and follow through.

7. *Fifty Percent of Success Could Be Just Showing Up*: Reliability is key to keeping and winning over customers. Don't you hate it when the plumber, the electrician, or the AC repairperson is late or, worse, never comes when you have a problem? Be the exception in today's world: show up and fix the problem, and that will yield big dividends.

8. *First Impressions Are Critical to Great Interactions That Lead to Enhanced Client Relations*: Ensure that whoever is answering your phones, or whoever is the first person a customer meets at the reception desk, is someone trained to be polite, courteous, well spoken, and helpful. A sure sign of how the company is run appears when you walk into an office environment and an employee is chomping on a piece of gum, texting on his or her cell phone, and ignoring you until you have to practically pound your fist on the desk to get attention.

9. *You May Not Always Have the Answer Immediately, but Take the Time to Listen*: Ask questions, and see what body language says, along with tone of voice. Clearly, when people are upset, the last thing they want to hear is assumption as to what they want. Really hear what the issue is and see how you can work to resolve it. "My bad" isn't appropriate, but "I am very sorry; let me see what I can do to help you immediately" is.

10. *Be Grateful That You Have Great Customers and Clients*: After all, without them, it would be hard to make a living, support your family, and experience the things you love to do. Take time to appreciate that those who buy your products and services are making all of that possible. I never forget how important my clients are and never take them for granted. Showing your appreciation through great service allows your customers to trust you, and that is the basis for any great relationship.

7

The Triumph of Accountability

Be a yardstick of quality. Some people aren't used to an environment where excellence is expected.

—Steve Jobs

I t doesn't have to be this bad. Sure, some businesses are in it only for the money. They care more about profiting from than protecting their customers and typically end up failing at both. But not all corporations have their priorities wrong. Many have shown a willingness to stand up and be accountable. They have set high standards of performance and have consistently met them.

One of those dreadfully uncomfortable "Should I howl in derisive laughter or try to appear deeply pensive?" corporate moments...

Nordstrom was one of the pioneers in customer service excellence, with stories—like the one about the customer who returned a tire there even though Nordstrom has never sold tires—going viral even before the Internet was where such stories were told. Or car company Lexus, which handled the recall of its ES 350 in 2006 a little differently from how most automakers might—it scheduled appointments for repairs, and when the owners arrived, they were given brand new Lexuses to drive home. You've probably also heard of Ritz-Carlton's early efforts to track its customers' preferences to ensure that future stays were even more comfortable and subsequent stories regarding the lengths to which the company will go to serve its customers.

So what's so different about these high achievers? It's as simple as putting the customers' needs and wants first and doing everything they can to meet them. Period. None of the ifs, ands, or buts we're so used to hearing about what could have or should have happened. When faced with customer problems, they solve them.

CUSTOMER SERVICE ROLE MODELS

High atop the list of customer service kings and queens is relative newcomer Zappos. Since the company's founding in 1999, Zappos's culture and business processes have always been closely aligned with providing exceptional service to its customers. As CEO Tony Hsieh put it, "We believe that customer service shouldn't be just a department; it should be the entire company." While the world's top online shoe retailer's best-known products are shoes and boots, the company is actually providing a service, of which Hsieh is well aware. Some of the ways Zappos separates itself from its competition is free shipping both ways, meaning that if you order the wrong size or decide you really don't like the shoes that arrive, you can ship them back at no cost to you. L.L. Bean pioneered free shipping on all orders decades ago, but few other companies also pay for return shipments.

Zappos also has a 365-day return policy, not the seven- or 14-day return window that just about every other company on the planet offers. No need to rush on that return, it seems to suggest. However, when customers place orders and are promised their shoes in four or five days, Zappos almost always pays for faster shipping, to surprise and delight its customers. How many other companies place a priority on that?

To ensure it is providing the best quality of customer service possible, Zappos invests considerable time in hiring and training its call center team. But unlike other companies' call centers, which are transaction focused, Zappos's is all about getting customers what they need, no matter how long it takes. In fact, in 2012, Zappos reported a new record for the length of a single customer call: 10 hours and 29 minutes. And after more than 10 hours, how much had Zappos sold to that customer? One pair of Ugg boots. Zappos was thrilled. In fact, the company once considered outsourcing the call center to experts but decided against it in order to stay close to its customers. By keeping its center in-house, Zappos demonstrated that customer service is not just one department—it's indeed what the whole company is about.

By emphasizing a consultative selling approach by phone—helping customers get what they want, whether Zappos has it in stock or not—Zappos has reduced the amount of money it spends on advertising to almost zero. Said Hsieh in a *Harvard Business Review* interview: "Our philosophy has been that most of the money we might ordinarily have spent on advertising should be invested in customer service, so that our customers will do the marketing for us through word of mouth." Word-of-mouth referrals and praise for the quality of service have fueled growth at Zappos, where 75 percent of its business comes from repeat customers.

Research firm Forrester defines customer service as "the perception by customers that a firm does what's best for them, not just what's best for its own bottom line." I think that's an accurate description of what companies should strive to do and how customers themselves define customer service. A company that Forrester ranks very highly in customer service is GEICO insurance company, which is a subsidiary of Warren Buffett's Berkshire Hathaway.

They've certainly showed me great service. Our family was driving on a long road trip when a pebble struck the windshield and left a small crack. We called GEICO immediately, and the day I returned home, it had set up the windshield/glass repair people to come to my office. Within an hour, done! Oh, and by the way, a well-known car dealer wanted $1,300 for a windshield replacement. The same exact service from GEICO came to $100, the cost of the deductible.

Like Zappos, GEICO provides service to its customers 24-7, even on holidays. Also like Zappos, GEICO places great emphasis on training, especially in its phone centers, where most customer contact occurs. As a result, GEICO customers are quite happy with the treatment they receive and the product knowledge demonstrated by GEICO phone reps. Customers also appreciate the company's low rates and the availability of local agents.

All of these factors result in GEICO's receiving high marks for its customer service from its customers, 97 percent of whom are satisfied.

2014 CUSTOMER SERVICE
— HALL OF —
FAME

1	AMAZON.COM	"EXCELLENT" 57.5%
2	HILTON WORLDWIDE	"EXCELLENT" 41.4%
3	MARRIOTT INTERNATIONAL	"EXCELLENT" 39.9%
4	CHICK-FIL-A	"EXCELLENT" 38.6%
5	AMERICAN EXPRESS	"EXCELLENT" 37.7%
6	TRADER JOE'S	"EXCELLENT" 37.2%
7	UPS	"EXCELLENT" 36.7%
8	SONY	"EXCELLENT" 36.5%
9	HEWLETT-PACKARD	"EXCELLENT" 36.2%
10	APPLE	"EXCELLENT" 35.7%

USED WITH PERMISSION FROM 24/7 WALL STREET

In an industry such as insurance, that rating is quite remarkable. In J.D. Power's 2013 U.S. Auto Insurance Satisfaction Study, GEICO performed above average in every part of the country but one, placing it squarely in the top half of all companies overall. Insure.com's 2014 customer satisfaction survey of auto insurers ranked GEICO fourth in the nation, with 92 percent of its current customers indicating that they would renew their policy. The three firms that scored higher, USAA, State Farm, and Farmers, received total scores within three points of GEICO, suggesting only minor differences.

Because insurance payouts reduce a company's profits, customers are generally anxious when a claim needs to be made. However, GEICO's stellar finances seem to allay its customers' fears. The fact that it has an A++ rating must also be reassuring.

Of course, its credit rating is tied to its financial stability, which is strong and only getting stronger, thanks to continued growth and profitability. A report by *SNL Financial* stated that GEICO's direct personal auto premiums increased 11.3 percent to $18.56 billion in 2013, "the largest percentage increase of the top 20 personal auto insurers and GEICO's largest percentage of annual premium gain since 2005." Even more remarkable, said SNL Financial, was that the next-best year-over-year gain produced by a competitor was almost 200 basis points lower.

Another customer service standout has to be Apple, which is generally associated more with creativity and innovation than customer service but which deserves the accolades nonetheless. Because Apple approaches product design in order to achieve a positive customer service experience, it designs products that are easy to use and that in most cases are better than what is currently on the market. The company's fans are loyal and outspoken—another sign that it is serving its customer base well.

More recently, as in the past 10 years, Apple's growth strategy has shifted to retail as it has continued to open retail storefronts worldwide. There were plenty of skeptics before the first store opened and very few today, as even

Microsoft is now emulating the strategy by opening its own stores. Perhaps that's why Apple took the unusual step of patenting its store layout and design.

Apple retail stores are like playgrounds, where consumers can visit, play with the products, have all their questions answered by knowledgeable tech associates, or get technical support regarding a product they currently own. Apple Stores are arguably the most successful stores in the world today. They are certainly the most profitable, generating an astounding $5,600 per square foot. Yet Apple employees are trained not so much in sales but in providing a magical customer experience; a visit to an Apple Store is much more about interacting with the products than buying them.

Employees are empowered to do what's necessary to please the customer. In job interviews, candidates are evaluated based on their potential ability to provide customers with a "transformational experience." That's a pretty high bar, don't you think?

Apple doesn't. In *The Apple Experience*, author Carmine Gallo describes how Apple Store employees are trained and expected to treat store visitors. First and foremost, they are there to solve problems and answer questions. To do that, they share information, provide product tours, and suggest additional information, such as free Apple classes, to help customers make a purchase decision. Employees are not on commission, so whether the customer buys does not affect their paycheck, which is smart. But what Apple does better than most companies is ensure that employees thank visitors and give them a friendly good-bye and an invitation to return. That "fond farewell" serves Apple well, Gallo points out, because the feeling that customers have as they leave a business has a direct correlation with how positively they feel toward that company and how likely they are to return. Genius.

Apple's whole customer service strategy revolves around truly serving its customers by first figuring out what they need or are interested in and then offering information and resources. Customers typically walk away inspired and often positively predisposed toward Apple. Feeling valued and feeling heard are at the core of what customers hope to get from the companies with which they do business.

But perhaps my favorite customer service story occurred thanks to Morton's, the Steakhouse. Someone in Morton's social media department had a finger on the pulse when weary business consultant Peter Shankman tweeted that he'd love to be greeted at the airport with a juicy porterhouse steak from Morton's. In fact, his exact, tongue-in-cheek, tweet was: "Hey, @ Mortons—can you meet me at Newark airport with a porterhouse when I land in two hours? K, thanks. :)." Then he probably fell asleep on the last leg of his journey home to New York.

What he probably never guessed was that Morton's in New York City saw that tweet and decided to honor his request. The restaurant did a little research to find out what airline Shankman was on and when and where he would arrive and then cooked up a delicious 24-ounce porterhouse, complete with sides of shrimp, potatoes, and bread, and had a tuxedoed gentleman drive the order 23.5 miles to hand it to Shankman, who was flabbergasted—and delighted. That's how you make a customer for life. And when that customer tells the tale to his circle of friends, you attract plenty of new customers as well.

Sure, these are the superstars of customer service, the companies that put the customer experience above all else in the hierarchy of priorities. But even companies that screw up can redeem themselves. In fact, companies that make mistakes or face difficulties and face them head-on can end up building almost impenetrable customer relationships.

COMPANIES THAT CORRECTED COURSE AND ARE SUCCEEDING

My local Mercedes-Benz dealership is one such example. When I started looking at cars a few years ago, I stopped in to the dealership to check out the Mercedes models. I was surprised that I was completely ignored—not just once but several times. I started to wonder whether it was because I was a woman. No one acknowledged me when I stepped into the dealership, and even when I expressed interest, I received no follow-up later. As far as I could see, the customer service process was nonexistent.

Several years later, a client recommended the dealership. I told my story of being ignored, and the client assured me that things had changed and that I wouldn't be disappointed. So I gave the dealership another try. I was pleasantly surprised; the service was phenomenal.

The entire customer service department had been given a face-lift, from the interior layout to the process through which customers were greeted at the door and escorted in to the cushy waiting area. The attitude of all the employees was friendly and welcoming, like night and day compared to my miserable first visit. And now I'm a loyal customer to that dealership. In fact, the salesman who helped me even receives information when my car is in for service and calls me to see if everything is OK. This may be a CRM program, but it's working.

I understand that Mercedes-Benz as a company has made a commitment to improving customer satisfaction, through its Customer One program. CEO Steve Cannon has stated that customer satisfaction is the brand's first priority, and he seems to be taking a hard line with dealerships that are not meeting certain performance levels. In April 2014, the company paid out $40 million to the top 70 percent of its 340 dealerships as a bonus for superior customer service ratings; 70 dealerships received no bonus money at all as a way to incentivize them to up their game.

Mercedes has also spent $40 million on 10 different programs over the past few years in order to improve its customer satisfaction metrics, but it has achieved only partial success. A spring 2014 *Automotive News* report stated that "despite several dealer training programs in recent years, Mercedes moved up only one spot—to No. 8—in the 2014 J.D. Power Customer Satisfaction Index survey."

Cannon also believes customer service will be "the next major battlefield for all luxury manufacturers" and has vowed to put Mercedes on top. Because improved customer satisfaction is tied directly to sales and profitability, he's making it worth the dealerships' time by sharing the wealth that results from their customer focus. And customers like me are noticing.

JetBlue Airways customers are also starting to see a change in how the airline treats its customers. Founded in 1998, the relatively new airline was established to "bring the humanity back to air travel." And for several years it did, offering lower-cost travel without a sacrifice to service. Then in 2007, a huge winter storm severely damaged JetBlue's customer service reputation.

On Valentine's Day a few years ago, 10 JetBlue planes were essentially iced in on the runway at JFK International Airport in New York City. About half of the airline's 500 flights that day were canceled, which was an inconvenience, but those truly inconvenienced were the passengers who were stuck on planes for as long as 11 hours. Some were passengers trying to take off for another destination, such as a honeymoon in Aruba, and others were passengers who had arrived home to New York but who were not permitted to deplane until hours later. Customers, who felt like hostages, and airline industry analysts were up in arms about what JetBlue forced its passengers to endure.

Coining the phrase "Jet Black and Blue" for their mistreatment, passengers and some Washington lawmakers began a push for a new passenger bill of rights, to avoid a similar situation in the future. Fortunately, JetBlue was already ahead of them. Less than a week later, the company announced the JetBlue Customer Bill of Rights. More than anything, it was a promise that if customers are inconvenienced by JetBlue, a compensation program will be in place to reimburse those passengers anywhere from $25 for a delay of up to 30 minutes to a free round-trip airline ticket if the delay lasts several hours. The passengers who had been stuck on February 14 were also compensated for their wait times, and founder and CEO David Neeleman publicly apologized, vowing to do better.

That promise was a pivotal turning point for JetBlue, and while Neeleman was replaced just three months later, the airline has worked hard to repair its damaged reputation. Those efforts have been successful, as suggested by the results of the 2014 American Customer Satisfaction Index, which rank JetBlue number one in customer satisfaction for the third straight year.

Another company that stumbled but has since recovered is JPMorgan Chase, which *Forbes* referred to as "the nation's strongest, safest bank" not long ago. Then the "London Whale" fiasco occurred. A single trader in the company's London office lost $6.2 billion through trades that were poorly monitored. That was followed by a loss in court costing an additional $107.5 million that had to be returned to MF Global as part of a settlement. Yes, the money lost was big, but perhaps even bigger was JPMorgan Chase's loss of its once-revered reputation. For years, CEO Jamie Dimon could seemingly do no wrong. So when questions started to emerge about the bad trades, Dimon did himself and his employer no favors by trying to minimize the situation, referring to it as a "tempest in a teapot." Unfortunately, as he tried to downplay the severity of what had occurred, his comments served only to alarm the Securities and Exchange Commission and a number of U.S. lawmakers. Instead of being invited to Washington to be wined and dined, as he had been several times before, this time Dimon was called on the carpet and grilled for his company's poor oversight and internal practices.

And if Dimon had done what some other CEOs typically do, again denying serious problems or pointing fingers elsewhere, JPMorgan Chase may have suffered tremendous consequences. Fortunately, he did the exact opposite—he was honest.

Two months after the "tempest in a teapot" characterization of the situation, Dimon gave an extremely humble apology in which he highlighted his own errors. He started off by stating, "When I made that statement, I was dead wrong." How often do we hear such direct admissions as this? Hardly ever. Other admissions included "This is a terrible mistake . . . [it] should never have happened . . . I can't justify it" and admitting the trades were "flawed, complex, poorly reviewed, poorly executed, and poorly monitored." In his annual letter to shareholders, Dimon said, "Let me be direct . . . The London Whale was the stupidest and most embarrassing situation I have ever been a part of."

The financial losses for the company were massive and continued to impact its performance even in to 2014, when its first-quarter losses of $20 billion—thanks to 2013 legal settlements made—were the equivalent of a year's worth of profits. Despite those losses, JPMorgan Chase has continued to focus on its customer and in 2014 was the bank category winner in the 2014 Brand Keys Customer Loyalty Engagement Index.

My own experience with American Express underscores how companies can turn dissatisfied customers into loyal ones fairly easily. When my American Express card was compromised, the company called to alert me and to immediately cancel my card. The fact that it was on top of the situation was comforting, and I was assured that I would receive a new card via overnight delivery. Well, the card didn't show up, so I called to follow up on where it was. The rep I spoke with didn't have an answer for me, but I was told I would receive a call back right away. Then nothing. It wasn't until several days later that I received a call back from American Express, and this time the service rep was very apologetic, admitted the company had screwed up, and attempted to make reparations by giving me 12,000 American Express membership reward points.

While the points didn't erase the inconvenience of not having an active card for several days, they did demonstrate that American Express knew it had provided poor service and wanted to make it up to me. Given that I can convert those points into things I use regularly, they were worth something to me. More importantly, American Express showed me that it values me as a customer. It failed in its initial customer service attempt and was doing its best to rectify the situation. It gets points for that.

Unfortunately, consumers have come to expect poor service. It's a given, we think, and when we have a problem with a product or service, we start the conversation ready for a fight. As previously referenced, that's what happened when a colleague of mine brought a humidifier back to P.C. Richard a year after it was purchased, complaining that it had completely died. He dreaded having to explain what happened and demand a refund or replacement. He knew he likely wouldn't get it, since he had used it for a full year, but on principle, he was ready to ask. So he walked in to the store and asked to see a manager.

When the manager came out, my colleague briefly stated what happened and waited for pushback. He got none. The manager immediately offered to replace it, no questions asked—really—and apologized for the problem. My colleague was stunned—pleased but stunned that there was no need for threats or social media complaints or calls to the regional manager to get the situation resolved. Within about five seconds, he had his problem taken care of.

Isn't it sad that we have become so conditioned to expect a fight when we are dissatisfied with what a company has sold us? We expect that someone will tell us "too bad" and walk away—probably because that happens the majority of the time. That needs to change. We shouldn't assume we will walk away dissatisfied. Because the truth is satisfying customers is good business.

Making customer service a company's top priority has repeatedly been shown to rectify past errors, no matter how huge. Companies that commit to working both on internal controls, as JPMorgan Chase, JetBlue, and Mercedes-Benz have, and on customer satisfaction can make impressive strides in a relatively short amount of time.

Companies can turn their fortunes around fairly quickly by recommitting to do their best for their customers.

THE IMPACT OF CUSTOMER SERVICE

Good or bad, quality of customer service has been shown to determine a company's profitability and level of success. And by most accounts, improving quality of service has a positive effect on nearly every aspect of a company's operations. One oft-used statistic from Bain has stuck with me: increasing customer retention rates by 5 percent increases profits by 25–95 percent, as reported in a 2002 *Harvard Business Review* article. Another Bain finding is that a 10 percent increase in customer retention levels (generally associated with high customer satisfaction) results in a 30 percent increase in the value of the company.

That's huge, don't you think? Holding on to 10 percent more of your customers, through improved quality and service, increases the value of your company by 30 percent. If that doesn't underscore the value of customer satisfaction, I don't know what will.

Similarly, data from the Gartner Group and *Leading on the Edge of Chaos* reported that companies that prioritize the customer experience earn 60 percent higher profits than companies that don't.

Given the statistics indicating how important customer service is to revenue and profitability, it's surprising, to me at least, how few companies invest time in determining how best to improve their customers' experience. If that's the key to enhanced customer satisfaction, I would think businesses would be more fixated on strategizing how best to make changes. Yet only 26 percent of companies have a well-developed strategy in place for improving the customer experience, according to the Econsultancy MultiChannel Customer Experience Report.

So the fact that the RightNow Customer Experience Impact Report found that 89 percent of consumers have stopped doing business with a company after experiencing poor customer service is no surprise. Their biggest reason for defecting? Indifference, believe it or not. The Customer Thermometer reports that 68 percent of customers leave because they "perceive you are indifferent to them." So you don't even have to give bad customer service; you just have to make the customer feel unappreciated. I think that's important to understand. Giving attention to customers can determine how satisfied they are with you.

Of course, customers who are dissatisfied let everyone know it. Customers who had a bad experience will tell 22 people they know, whereas customers who were happy with how they were treated will tell only nine, found AllBusiness.com. That means you have to delight three customers to compensate for or overcome that one dissatisfied customer.

Now, all this data about the importance of providing excellent customer service apparently does not apply in industries with a monopoly, such as cable television service, local phone service, or the U.S. Postal Service. According to the American Customer Satisfaction Index: "Industries where competition is limited—including virtual monopolies like the U.S. Postal Service's mail delivery—generally show lower satisfaction overall. The airline industry with its hub structure or cable TV with its service area limitations are good examples of poor customer satisfaction."

Frustrating as it may be, *Bloomberg Businessweek* reported that "the most-hated companies perform better than their beloved peers." The primary reason seems to be that the companies have little incentive at all to try to satisfy customers; in fact, investing time and money to that goal may simply be wasteful. So they may not. And profits result.

That's the bad news. The good news is that few companies operate in a monopoly, meaning that the vast majority of us have great incentives to do all that we can to satisfy our customers. And most of us are taking steps to improve customer service and customer satisfaction.

THE RISING IMPORTANCE OF CUSTOMER EXPERIENCE

Customer service and customer satisfaction are some of the biggest factors in the customer experience (CX), which is where many larger companies are increasingly investing their money, says a 2013 study by the Temkin Group. Temkin reported that 63 percent of large companies (greater than $500 million in annual revenue) surveyed in the fourth quarter of 2013 said they expect to spend "significantly" or "somewhat more" on customer experience this year. That 63 percent is an increase from 54 percent that planned those increases in 2012 and from 46 percent in 2011.

Another trend that has emerged and has been building momentum since 2006 is the creation of a customer advocate position at the senior management level. Most commonly called the Chief Customer Officer (CCO), these newly created positions are responsible for keeping customer satisfaction on the companies' radars; other variations of the title are the Chief Client Officer and the Chief Experience Officer. Organizations ranging from Allstate and Dunkin' Brands to USAA and even Girl Scouts of the USA all have hired CCOs.

The creation of the CCO position seems to be spurred by one or more of the following situations, according to *Forbes*: "a change in leadership, a desire to accelerate growth, a reaction to competitive forces, and a response to changes brought about by rapid growth." I think the question that remains is whether these new roles will appreciably alter how companies go about giving customers their best or whether they are a short-term initiative that will be replaced in a couple of years with some new approach.

Either way, shining a spotlight on the need to take responsibility for excellent customer service is a good thing. It puts competitive pressure on all industry participants to up their game, to provide their customers with quality products and services. Those organizations that are taking shortcuts or putting profits above their customers' welfare can be pressured out.

Companies that are smart routinely study their competition. They know what everyone is up to and look for best practices that can be applied in their own organizations. Smart companies are also transparent to their customers and tell them what they are doing to ensure customer safety; they talk less about performance and more about protection and responsibility. They also have explicit quality assurance programs and internal processes established to keep the public safe from harm or wrongdoing. And when issues of customer service or poor performance come up, they emphasize their own track record of success so as to distance themselves from the others.

To achieve improvements in customer service, customer satisfaction, and customer experience, as I've said before, we need to go back to the fundamentals. Treating customers the way you would want to be treated is one step away from mediocrity and toward top quality. Be honest. Be polite. Do what you say you'll do. Demonstrate that your business is trustworthy. The process is fairly straightforward, but it certainly isn't easy. The right way is almost always the hard way, isn't it?

10 TIPS FOR IMPROVING THE CUSTOMER EXPERIENCE

You've read here about customer experience role models—companies that are taking seriously the importance of providing excellent service throughout the entire purchase process. Here are 10 things you can do now to ensure that your organization is providing a superior customer experience.

1. *Focus on Consistency*: Providing a top-quality product or service once is much easier than providing your customers with a quality experience every single time. This is what frequently trips businesses up: their internal processes don't support ongoing consistency throughout the customers' experience. Take a look at your product or service and how it is being marketed and delivered in order to identify opportunities for improvement.

2. *Be Transparent*: Customers value honesty and integrity, two qualities that can be easy to spot when companies are open about their practices and their products and services. Organizations that are quick to admit failure or to warn about harmful situations are much more reputable and trustworthy than those who are quiet—perhaps too quiet—and more likely to point fingers or deny any misdeeds. Being transparent increases customer trust, which enhances the customer experience.

3. *Invest in Training*: How your employees are trained directly impacts the quality of your customers' experience. The more training they receive, the more consistently your team can deliver excellence. Start at the point of first contact, which is often a receptionist, and research available training and personal development opportunities to improve everything from how the phone is answered, to how a transfer is made, to how long someone should stay on hold. Then move to the next point of contact and see what training might aid in improving the customers' experience with your company at that step. Training can significantly improve the quality of customer service you provide.

4. *Build in Follow-Up*: Where many companies often fall short in providing quality service is in the follow-up. Customers are left hanging, waiting for an answer or resolution to their situation, and many providers don't seem to care. Communication can solve so many customer complaints! So keep in touch at every step in the process, whether you're still gathering information on their behalf or you now have an answer. Let them know. Bad news should always travel faster than good news. If you anticipate a delay of some sort, let them know that as well. They may not be happy about it, but they will certainly be even less pleased if they're told nothing at all. Lack of information only generates more questions, more phone calls, more e-mails, and more complaints. Cut those down by following up and staying in touch.

5. *Make Customer Satisfaction the Hallmark of Your Company's Corporate Culture*: Communicating to employees the utmost importance of customer safety, security, and satisfaction can shape a corporate culture. Rather than emphasizing sales and profitability, talk more about customer service, quality work, and being a good corporate citizen. Aim to be known for delighted customers more than anything else.

6. *Take Pride in Your Workmanship*: You don't need to be a skilled artisan to take pride in what you do. Whether you're an accountant, a brand manager, or the owner of a corner bodega, you can strive to give it your all every day. Do you give your clients your best advice? Do you negotiate the very best deals for your clients at every opportunity? If you give your clients your best work, you have pride of workmanship. Don't take shortcuts.

7. *Make Reparations*: When you screw up or make a mistake and you recognize it, take the opportunity to apologize to your customers and make things right. That means reimbursing them in some way for their inconvenience or the poor service you provided. At the restaurant I previously mentioned, all we needed was for part of our meal to be taken off our bill because of the long wait. It wasn't about the money; it was about recognizing the issue, and prompt recognition of the issue would have dramatically changed how we felt as we left the place that night. JetBlue tried to compensate its stranded passengers with free flights and refunds. Figure out what you can do to show your customers that you recognize that they received poor service or that the product they purchased was defective in some way and to demonstrate that you care, that you want to keep them as customers, and that you are willing to invest in that relationship.

8. *Listen, Listen, Listen*: You will satisfy your customers' needs if you know what they need to begin with. Remember the acronym WIIFM; they'll be asking, "What's in it for me?" Anticipating what people need is not as good as *knowing* what they need. Because most people and companies have needs, finding what they are and being a resource for satisfying those needs are the keys to great business.

9. *Create the Opportunity to Provide More*: If your clients trust you, they will want more from you. Providing an "of counsel" approach especially if you are in a service business is what service providers strive for. There are no better words to your ears as a business owner or CEO than when someone asks, "What do you think I should do?" That shows you the trust they put in you, and that leads to greater and more expanded opportunities to grow your relationship. After all, people do business with people they like and trust.

10. *Exceed Expectations*: This is probably the most important tip for gaining new customers and clients and making people take notice. Remember the Morton's story or the one about P.C. Richard? Finding ways to make people do a double take and think, "Wow, I didn't expect that," is a perfect way to ensure repeat business and great word-of-mouth referrals.

8

In the End, It's All about People

The core of our success. That's the most difficult thing for a competitor to imitate. They can buy all the physical things. The things you can't buy are dedication, devotion, loyalty—the feeling that you are participating in a crusade.

—Herb Kelleher, Southwest Airlines
cofounder and former CEO

The days of the handshake deal may be over, but following through on what you promise others is as important as ever, from the little things to the big ones. Starting with an understanding that no one expects perfection, we can still strive for excellence rather than mediocrity. Providing superior customer service and quality products and services is still a reasonable goal and a reasonable expectation from our customers.

So how do you achieve excellence? It starts and ends with people. That translates into a focus on giving customers what they want, training employees to provide the best possible service, and fostering a corporate culture that values its workers and its customers.

PROVIDING THE HUMAN TOUCH

If you start with a desire for repeat business, not just one-time transactions, and build an organization around that pursuit of long-term customer relationships, you're on the right track as a company. Providing an excellent customer experience starts with knowing what customers want, striving to exceed their expectations, and adapting as those needs change.

It starts with contact. As we're finding out, consumers aren't really fans of the impersonal way most companies are communicating with them. While the trend in recent years has been toward increased customer contact, that contact is mainly impersonal and almost always through e-mail. Perhaps it's no shocker then that companies are starting to notice that frequency does not necessarily result in stronger customer relationships or increased sales— quite the opposite in some cases.

Marketing technology company Responsys reported that in 2011, the nation's top 100 online retailers sent individuals on their e-mail lists an average of 177 e-mails each, which is an increase of 87 percent from 2007. That's approximately an e-mail every other day. And those aren't even the more aggressive companies.

Neiman Marcus Group sent its list more than 500 e-mails, found Responsys, which means that some days their customers received multiple e-mail messages from the company. In a single day. Not surprisingly, customers are getting burned out from all this promotional e-mail cluttering their inboxes.

From 2007 to 2011, e-mail marketing firm Harte-Hanks found that customers opened fewer e-mails. During the first half of 2007, consumers opened 19 percent of the e-mails they received from retailers and clicked through to their websites 3.9 percent of the time. Those aren't great numbers, and they certainly don't suggest strong engagement. So when those numbers dropped to 12.5 and 2.8 percent respectively, by the same period in 2011, many companies began pulling back.

Online retailer Nicole Miller, for example, reduced the number of e-mails sent by 66 percent—from three per week to one—and saw its unsubscribes fall and its open rate increase from 15 to 40 percent. Sales from its e-mails also rose from 10 to 17 percent. Yes, sometimes there is such a thing as too much contact, especially when it lacks human touch. Smart companies that are seeing their open rates and sales fall as the number of e-mails sent rises are wisely cutting back on e-mail interactions.

The Corporate Executive Board study confirmed that, from a customer's perspective, interactions do not equal a relationship. Shared values are what drive relationships, respondents said. In the study, 64 percent of consumers cited shared values as the reason for their relationship with a brand. Far fewer—13 percent—cited frequent interactions as the basis for their relationship with a brand. So if you're relying too heavily on e-mail to stay top of mind with customers, consider cutting back on those outgoing e-mails; you may not be doing yourself or your customers any favors.

Interestingly, consumers are taking steps to make more human contact, not less. The trend is toward more time spent shopping within stores. A 2013 Nielsen study reported that, overall, consumers are making fewer shopping trips. This is a carryover from the recession of 2008 that continues to impact how and when consumers buy. However, the good news is that while they may visit fewer stores or shop less, consumers are spending more per trip.

Says Nielsen, the key is bringing the store to the consumers, wherever they are. That seems to be because customers prefer to deal with other people, not automated systems or websites. Research in 2012 from Forrester confirmed that customers want to deal with a live human being.

Forrester states, "The vast majority of customers actually prefer getting customer service in person or over the phone." So they like to research products and services online, but they prefer dealing with a live human being when it comes to actually buying something. Eighty-seven percent of consumers still prefer to buy in brick-and-mortar environments, presumably because of the human contact. That's an important piece of information if you're trying to satisfy your customers.

So wouldn't it make much more sense for car dealers, who are notorious for sending out follow-up e-mails or making phone calls the instant you walk out of the dealership, to inquire about the quality of service you *just* received before you walk out the door? Instead of scheduling an e-mail to be sent the second a customer's credit card is swiped to pay for the brake work she had done, how about having the service manager approach her and ask for a minute of her time? The quality and immediacy of the information the dealership gathers will be second to none, because it's fresh in its customer's mind and it doesn't require her to spend more time later answering questions. Given what we now know about consumer preference for human contact, wouldn't that be a better approach to customer satisfaction research?

Today, customers buy where they get the best products and services. Sure, they may research purchases on sites with a huge inventory selection, but they'll eventually buy from the company that provides them with the best overall value. Part of that value equation includes human interaction.

Studies show that consumers feel better about and trust companies that provide a live person to buy from at some point in that process. Being able to talk with a live person builds trust and preference, which may be why more online retailers are adding a live chat function so people can ask questions via instant message or are prominently featuring an 800 number on their home page in case customers have questions (well, unless you're

Amazon, which hides its phone numbers). Putting customers in touch with people helps provide excellent service and higher satisfaction.

THE IMPORTANCE OF "BRAND HUMANITY"

We need to add humanity back into the business process. So much is done online now in an impersonal, often anonymous environment that we seem to assume that it's for the better, that speed trumps all. Actually, it doesn't, and consumers are starting to recognize this and long for a return to a personal connection.

A new phrase is being circulated that gets at this need for human connection: "brand humanity." Malone and Fiske discuss its importance in their *Bloomberg Businessweek* column titled "The Importance of 'Brand Humanity' for Customer Loyalty," in which they state that demonstrating warmth and competence can lead to improved trust and increased sales.

The authors point to Domino's Pizza as a prime example of what warmth and an apology can do for a company. In late 2009, CEO Patrick Doyle took to TV commercials to personally apologize for the lackluster quality of Domino's pizza. He admitted it wasn't very good, told customers the chain's recipe had been significantly improved, and asked TV viewers to please give Domino's a second chance. The move was an unusual one, but it paid off.

Consumers responded to the humility Doyle showed. With that message and a personal appeal for help, Domino's witnessed the biggest growth in sales that quarter in the history of the fast-food industry. That's not just within the pizza industry but within the total fast-food world. Even today, Domino's sales figures continue to be strong.

Malone and Fiske explain that this is not surprising. Apparently, we all constantly evaluate each other on two key attributes: warmth and competence. We judge others on our assessments of the following questions, measuring warmth and competence, respectively: "What are the intentions of this other person toward me?" and "How capable is this person of carrying out those intentions?" At Domino's, the public got the sense that Doyle was sincere in his request for a second chance and that, as leader of the company, he had the power and authority to make needed changes. It was a home run.

Johnson & Johnson is another example of a company that stumbled and was able to right itself after expressing sincere remorse and a commitment to change. Not so much for Barilla and its CEO's antigay remarks or Lululemon's CEO Chip Wilson, who made derogatory comments about overweight women and racist comments about foreigners' ability to speak the letter *l*. Not surprisingly, Wilson's apology showed no warmth and little competence. Both companies have taken a major hit and don't seem to have a plan in place to humanize their cultures. Unfortunately, being their best is going to be hard when their leadership shows such poor judgment. Cleaning house, as Lululemon did by replacing its CEO, may be the only way out.

Companies that are thriving are investing more in communicating directly with their customers. Malone and Fiske point to Honest Tea, Panera Bread, and Chobani yogurt as examples of companies that are demonstrating warmth and competence through their brands. What separates these companies is their willingness to put the customer first and to let them know it, by thought, word, and deed.

What researchers have found is that consumers attribute human characteristics to brands and judge them as they do other people. So when brands, or companies, are forthright and trustworthy, consumers like them more, just as they would people. Or when they ask for forgiveness, they're likely to give it to them if they come across as sincere. But warmth and competence are the two main points when it comes to assessments. According to 2011 research by Susan Fiske and Nicolas Kervyn of Princeton University, "Over 50 percent of purchase and loyalty behavior across a host of categories can be explained by customers' warmth and competence assessments and the resulting emotions they elicit." That's where we really need to focus our attention if we want to connect with customers and discover new and better ways to serve them.

Because that's what all this research is about, isn't it? It's about learning more about customers so we can deliver products and services they need in a way that best satisfies them. Giving our customers our best requires that we actually get to know them. Then, check in with them every six months or so, to see how well you're satisfying their needs and whether you could do anything better. Don't inundate them with weekly SurveyMonkey surveys, but ask them to grade you twice a year—that's not too much. Then listen.

FINDING THE RIGHT PEOPLE TO DELIVER EXCELLENT SERVICE

Obviously, the responsibility for excellence rests in your employees' hands, as it always has. To provide the best products and services possible, you need to have the right people in place. At every step, you need the best—from research and product development to prototyping, testing, marketing, sales, and after-sales service.

Your employees also need to understand that the customers' needs come first—that everything else is immaterial. That means that senior management needs to model that customer-centric behavior, too, in order to create a culture that celebrates the customer . . . and let it cascade down through the organization.

Employees also need to trust those above them on the org chart. Transparency needs to come from the top down, so that everyone inside and outside the organization trusts that he or she knows the state and intentions of the organization. That transparency results in more confident, proud employees who don't spend part of their day wondering whether they're next on the chopping block (because they know how things are going). And customers don't harbor fear that you haven't told them everything they need to know about their recent purchase.

Transparency is at the root of excellence. When backed up with policies that demonstrate how essential your customers are—individually—to the company, you have a powerful corporate culture. One company that does an excellent job of helping employees understand the importance of their work for customers is Celgene.

Celgene, based in New Jersey, has been atop the "Business Insider's Best Employers in America" list for the past two years. Ninety-one percent of the company's employees are highly satisfied with their work, which is developing and commercializing therapies to treat cancer and other inflammatory diseases. The reason for such a sense of fulfillment likely comes down to how connected Celgene workers are to the good their products can do and the difference they can make in their customers' lives. Celgene employees regularly have the opportunity to interact with the very patients who are benefiting from the company's work, which 93 percent of employees find meaningful. Said Celgene President Alan Colowick, MD, "Each of us comes to work every day understanding our unique role and firmly believing that we not only can make a difference but we make the difference to patients every day, worldwide." That's pretty powerful.

The company's marketing backs up that patient focus, too. The message inside and outside Celgene is that patient health comes first. The customer comes first (just look at the website, www.celgene.com). No wonder it is ranked number one.

Now contrast this commitment to improving customers' lives with GM's treatment of its own internal whistleblowers. Celgene asks for its employees' help in "monitoring and reporting on the safe use of our products," while GM tried to keep its own employees quiet when trouble is identified. In fact, Courtland Kelley, the former head of a nationwide GM inspection program on the Cobalt and a GM employee for more than 30 years, said he "found flaws [on GM vehicles] and reported them, over and over, and repeatedly found his colleagues' and supervisors' responses wanting. He thought they were more concerned with maintaining their bureaucracies and avoiding expensive recalls than with stopping the sale of dangerous cars." His concerns about his employer's products were swept under the rug and ignored for years. He even filed a lawsuit in 2002 to bring attention to safety issues surrounding the Cobalt's predecessor, the Cavalier, to no avail. It wasn't until years later that Kelley's observations came to light and put GM in the hot seat. Now CEO Mary Barra is working to change the culture that allowed this to happen.

What brought these incidents to the fore was an internal investigation commissioned by GM itself. The results were published in a document known as the Valukas report, after the former U.S. attorney who prepared it. What Valukas found was evidence of a corporate culture gone bad, as far as GM's customers were concerned. Instead of putting consumer safety as job one, cover-ups and secrecy were tantamount. Said the report, "Group after group and committee after committee within GM that reviewed the issue failed to take action or acted too slowly. Although everyone had responsibility to fix the problem, nobody took responsibility."

And if that weren't bad enough, it became clear that employees were "actively discouraged" from speaking up about defects or concerns and that those who did, like Kelley, "could derail their careers."

GM's culture reportedly is one of secrecy and CYA behavior that does not build trust internally or with customers. It is not a culture of excellence by any stretch, which is why improving customer satisfaction is going to be an uphill battle. In contrast, Celgene doesn't have that problem.

Celgene's culture of excellence makes it easier to retain quality employees, and because it focuses on treating people well inside and out, attracting potential employees is much easier, too. Celgene is an easy sell to potential employees. Talent acquisition costs are lower because of the company's quality reputation; people *want* to work there.

The challenge is retaining that top talent once hired. Companies that treat their employees well will have low turnover and high customer satisfaction.

KEEPING TOP TALENT

While branding is important, hiring the right employees is even more so. Finding employees who fit the company, its mission, its customers, and its corporate culture is critical to the success of any organization. Charles Ellis, in his book *What It Takes: Seven Secrets of Success from the World's Greatest Professional Firms*, reports that "the best in the business"—whatever industry we're talking about—are "fanatical about recruiting new employees who are not just the most talented but also the best suited to a particular corporate culture." He gives the example of consulting firm McKinsey, which interviews 200,000 people each year and selects only 1 percent as new hires. Marissa Mayer, CEO of Yahoo!, reportedly reviews the résumés of every new hire candidate (which I think is quite a challenge, given all the demands on her time and the fact that she has 15,000 employees), but that level of involvement shows how important finding the right people is to each organization. We all need to be that picky.

We also need to hire more for potential than for the particular skills applicants have today. Research from Leadership IQ in 2012 reported that 46 percent of new hires will fail within 18 months but only 11 percent failed because they lacked technical skills. Of those who failed, 26 percent were not coachable, 17 percent failed due to lack of motivation, and 15 percent failed due to temperament. Many factors more important than current technical skills are worth considering when evaluating employees.

One company that has a long-standing reputation for hiring for attitude and not technical training or know-how is Southwest Airlines. Southwest understands that it can teach most skills but it can't teach attitude. That's not to say that technical training isn't important, only that companies can provide it once applicants are hired. The Container Store, for example, which has been on *Fortune*'s "Best Companies to Work For" for 15 years, provides first-year full-time employees with 263 hours of training. This is approximately 256 hours more than the average retail employer offers. Not only does the Container Store thereby ensure that its employees are better able to assist customers but also annual turnover is only 10 percent, versus 100 percent industry-wide.

Obviously, the Container Store recognizes that what matters most to its customers is "knowledgeable staff," which is also what survey respondents told MSN/Zogby mattered to them as part of a customer service study. Consumers want employees who know what they're doing—no surprise there. That's why training is essential for companies interested in demonstrating customer service excellence.

Another example of a company that invests in its employees is Jiffy Lube, which earned the number one spot on *Training* magazine's top 125 list in 2014. Jiffy Lube is the poster child for aligning corporate goals with customer service and employee training. In addition to achieving a 900 percent increase in the number of its franchises at 100 percent certification, Jiffy Lube also saw its employee turnover rate decline and its franchisee approval rating hit 93 percent. Perhaps more important, however, is that "Jiffy Lube has experienced eight consecutive years of increased average revenue per customer and improved customer service scores." Investing in its people yields happier employees *and* customers.

The importance of training, education, and professional development is a message that needs to come from the top down. Corporate leaders and their priorities define a company's culture, for better or worse.

To be your best and to do your best to satisfy your customers, an executive team needs to first make it a priority. Once they've made it clear organization-wide that excellence is expected, excellence is what they will get. Conveying warmth and competence in their interactions with the organization and its customers will also enhance the brand image and reinforce its priorities. Refusing to tolerate "my bad" is a huge first step toward getting everyone's best.

Employees are much more likely to publicly declare their pride for their company when they trust their company's leaders. According to the Social

Workplace Trust Study, as reported in *Forbes*, employees are three times more likely to share information about their companies on social media and express pride about working there when they feel that their corporate leaders are trustworthy. Not only do trustworthy companies benefit from more love from their employees but also they have less difficulty attracting new employees. A 2014 Employer Branding Study by Randstad US found that the number one trait workers look for in an employer is honesty. In fact, there is an increasing emphasis on honesty as a competitive differentiator.

Don Peppers and Martha Rogers write in their book *Extreme Trust: Honesty as a Competitive Advantage* that the risk of negative repercussions from even one misstep has become so great, thanks to social media, that companies are shifting to proactively protecting customer interests. Otherwise, that one incident involving a new and uninformed employee can be your downfall.

Customers today are quick to rush online to report a company's mistake or poor service because they know social media mentions get attention, both from the company and from the public. Said Chris Malone and Susan Fiske in a 2013 *Bloomberg Businessweek* column, "Now the Internet, social networks, and mobile devices offer customers near-instantaneous power to pass judgment on how companies and brands conduct themselves. This has brought back the kind of social accountability in business that hasn't been seen since before the Industrial Revolution." Complain to a representative by phone and you'll most likely hear excuses but no action, but complain on Twitter and you'll get an immediate response and resolution. Because of these "rising levels of transparency," as Peppers and Rogers call it, companies are being pressured into providing better customer service. I'm not sure that's a bad thing, to be honest. If the threat of a poor online review is what's needed to get a business to shape up and provide better goods and services, I'd call that a move in the right direction.

Being able to adapt as the market shifts and customer needs change has long been associated with financial success. Corporate cultures that value employees, customers, and members of the community and are able to adapt to changing customer demands are more successful. So how do you start making that shift from mediocre to excellent?

WHERE TO START

I've given you a lot of tips throughout this book. Many are commonsense but most are not commonplace. These aren't new ideas, but someone needs to restart the dialogue, to get companies talking about giving customers their best. After all, don't they deserve it? And in turn I believe employees will give their best to their corporations and management. I was once at a human resources conference where HR professionals agreed that there is no loyalty on the part of either corporations or employees. Opening up the dialogue could just help change that.

So here are some questions to ask yourself, to guide you in creating a culture of excellence that attracts top talent and keeps them engaged in providing quality service, so that customers receive the best service possible:

- How are the demographic shifts occurring affecting our ability to hire the best?
- How are workforce changes impacting our recruitment efforts?
- How can I make my workplace environment more inviting and accommodating for employees?
- How do I continue to evolve my corporate environment on an ongoing basis to attract the best and the brightest?
- How am I currently showing respect and appreciation for my employees?
- Are we evaluating our work product routinely?
- Am I constantly looking for opportunities to build employee skills?
- Are we hiring for potential or for skills, and how do we shift that thinking?

- What can I do to help our employees grow and develop new skills and talents?
- Am I doing enough to engage employees, to encourage them to speak up and become part of the conversation about customer satisfaction and service?
- Do our employees know that I care about them? How?
- Have we created a culture of camaraderie and involvement?

Although we focus our time and attention on customers, the truth is that it's our workforce that is customer-facing and our employees who will determine how well we are meeting the needs of our customers. We need employees with potential and attitude to be the best company that we can be—because the company with the best talent is certainly a much stronger, much more successful company, no matter how you look at it.

Let's get rid of "my bad" and focus on "my best." I think Joan Rivers nailed it when she said, "Always shoot for the stars because you may only get the roof. If you shoot for the roof, you might just get the cellar." In my life I've always tried to shoot for the stars.

About the Author

Julie B. Kampf helps *Fortune* 500 companies and other organizations build high-performance teams that increase business success. As founder and CEO of the award-winning executive talent solutions firm JBK Associates International, she has worked with industry-leading companies and thousands of senior executives to provide a full range of services related to acquiring, retaining, and developing top talent. As a speaker and author, she challenges businesses to create more effective and inclusive leadership through her appearances in forums such as the Multicultural Forum on Workplace Diversity, the Linkage Summit on Leading Diversity, the Healthcare Businesswomen's Association Annual Conference, and *Profiles in Diversity Journal* and *Diversity Executive* to name a few. Kampf launched JBK in 2003 as a firm that defies industry norms by treating clients, candidates, and employees with deep respect, and she has established the company as one that competes with the biggest in its field, ranked among the nation's top 10 innovators in diversity by *Profiles in Diversity Journal,* as one of *Working Mother* magazine's top 25 Best Woman-Owned Companies, and as one of the *Inc.* 500|5000 fastest-growing private companies in America for three consecutive years. She also channels her passion for helping others succeed into her work as a career coach and industry mentor, as well as through her deep commitment to community service and philanthropy, which is one of her firm's founding principles. Twice named one of the 100 most inspiring people in the life sciences industry by *PharmaVOICE* magazine, Kampf strives daily to walk her talk as a strong mentor, a compassionate leader, and a citizen who gives back.

jbkassociates.net
Twitter.com/JBK_Associates
Facebook.com/jbkassociates